ATHONITE FATHERS
OF THE 20TH CENTURY
VOLUME 1

Athonite Fathers
of the 20ᵗʰ Century
Volume 1

CELL OF THE RESURRECTION
The Holy Mountain

UNCUT MOUNTAIN PRESS

ATHONITE FATHERS OF THE 20ᵀᴴ CENTURY
Volume 1

uncutmountainpress.com

Cover Design by George Weis.
Front cover: the Sacred Monastery of Karakallou.
Back cover: Elder Philaret of Karoulia.

Scriptural quotations from the Old Testament are translated from the Septuagint; from the New Testament, quotations are primarily taken from the King James Version. Some quotes have been emended to better reflect the Greek text.

Translated from the Greek text *From the Ascetic and Hesychastic Athonite Tradition.*

Library of Congress Cataloging-in-Publication Data
Cell of the Resurrection, Athos

Athonite Fathers of the 20ᵗʰ Century: Volume One – 1ˢᵗ ed.

ISBN: 978-1-63941-012-5

I. Christianity - Eastern Orthodox
II. Spirituality - Eastern Orthodox

"Many were persuaded to choose
the solitary life; and so henceforth
there arose monasteries even in the
mountains, and the desert was made a
city by monks coming out from their
own and enrolling themselves in the
heavenly citizenship."

— From the *Life of Saint Anthony*

CONTENTS

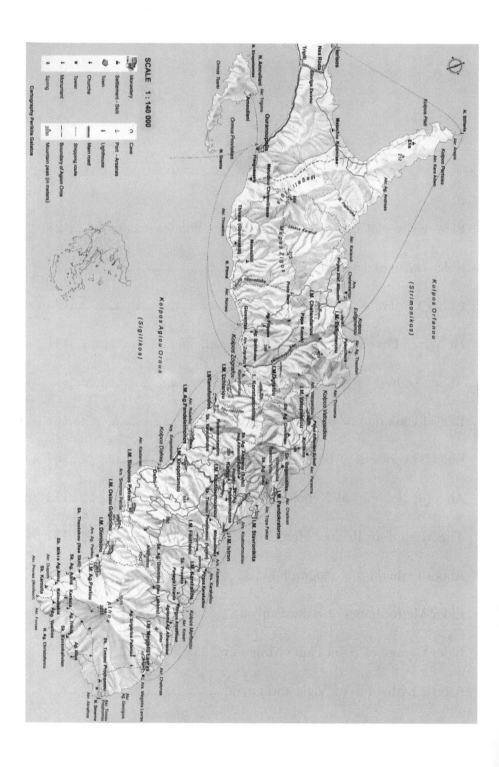

Prolegomenon
to the Greek Edition

The Holy Mountain of Athos is a symbol of love, of the monks' total dedication to God, and of the piety of the faithful Roman emperors, who endowed it with self-governance, inaccessibility (*abaton*), and many other related privileges. It still remains a living remnant of the sometime mighty and brilliant Roman "Byzantine" Empire. Its spiritual contribution throughout the ages has been immense and incalculable.

Despite the trials that it has undergone, the Holy Mountains remains unchanged, and in fact in our days it becomes more well-known and attracts more pilgrims. "In the last days the mountain of the Lord shall be conspicuous"; because the world has need of it, it is preserved by the grace of God and by the intercessions of the Lady Theotokos.

During its history the Holy Mountain was shaken by pirates' raids, by centuries-long barbarian occupation, by a lack of men, by a lack of material goods, by nationalistic conflicts, by theological and dogmatic controversies, and countless other sufferings. Today by the grace of God all these have vanished and the only danger threatening the Holy Mountain is a lack of fidelity to tradition. This living ascetical and hesychastic Athonite traditon, which is experienced as a way of life, of asceticism, and of worship for so many centuries, in every form of monastic life and by so great a multitude of monks, renders the Holy Mountain unique and unrepeatable.

Yet unfortunately today this so valuable Athonite tradition is going through a great crisis and is in danger of becoming changed by the worldly mindset and the many worldly comforts and influences.

There are traditions of many kinds on the Holy Mountain: architectural, musical, typical (of the typicon of the services), iconographical, et. al. They are all respected and considerable, but here we are referring to the lived experience of the ascetical and hesychastic tradition. This does not depend upon external manners and places nor is it exhausted in them. In other words, as many as live in the desert are ascetics and hesychasts, since asceticism and hesychia are mainly a spiritual state, achievement, and struggle. As many as are violent toward their nature and have watchfulness and prayer live this tradition, regardless of whether they exercise asceticism in a cell or in a cenobium. That is why this book does not present the tradition of one elder,[1] of one cell, or of some monastery, but the one, single, continuous, living, and variform tradition of the entirety of the Holy Mountain.

This lived Athonite tradition and the monastic schema make us similar to our predecessors and spiritually connect us to the holy Athonite fathers. This good, ascetical leaven remakes our earthen dough unto sanctification, since "asceticism is the mother of sanctification".[2] This is what gives us wings that we might rise spiritually. The Athonite tradition is the underground water which secretly irrigates and nourishes Athonite monasticism. It is the clear oxygen that quickens it. It is the unifying power that supports the Athonite

---

1   A note on the word "elder": In the present translation we have followed the English rules of capitalization, which do not always correspond to the Greek usage. The reader ought to bear in mind that "*geron*," "*geronda*", and especially the combining form "*gero-*" (all of which are rendered herein as "elder"), besides the reverential meaning of one spiritually advanced or a spiritual guide, also have the much more literal sense of "old man" (which is also the literal meaning of the English "elder") and are often so used to refer to an older monk, without necessarily implying an elevated spiritual state. So "*gero*-Macarius" on p.185 has been translated as "Elder Macarius" but could equally have been "Ol' Macarius". —ED.

2   The Ascetical Homilies of St. Isaac the Syrian, Ch. 16.

republic. It is the guarantee that we are on the right path. It is the continuation of our monastic life.

The monastic, traditional spirit with the ascetical way of life have the ability to restore monasticism and show forth new holy fathers. Without this life-creating spirit we are bones dead and lifeless. Likewise, if the buildings and relics are preserved but the monastic tradition is lost with the confinement of worship to a formal act, the Holy Mountain will have become a remarkable museum with cassock-wearing keepers.

Of course, the most honourable relics that exist on the Holy Mountain are the "living relics", the virtuous ascetics who are the bearers and expressors of the Athonite tradition.

The monastic life is like unto some Athonite flowers. They flourish in waterless places, they sprout between the stones of the benches and even high up on the towers of the monasteries, where there is not a drop of humidity, and yet, when they bloom, their fragrance is intoxicating. Many took seeds and cultivated these flowers out in the world in fertile gardens, watering them and fertilising them abundantly, but unfortunately they lost their fragrance. The same also happens with the monks. As much as they are deprived of worldly things and comforts, so much they become rich in spiritual things. As much as they live ascetically in the disconsolate desert without earthly and human consolations, so much are they nourished and fed by the heavenly and divine ones. That is why they are then fragrant with virtue and holiness. When we seek to turn the roughness of asceticism into smoothness and the strait way into a wide one, then we monks shall also become like unto the flowers that have lost their fragrance.

The old fathers, eponymous and anonymous, important and obscure, newer and older, who are mentioned in the following pages, had received little education or were even wholly illiterate, and some of them became monks out of incidental renunciation. Some of them were orphaned from a young age, became widowers in marriage, or found themselves in danger in the war and vowed, if they were saved, to become monks. And yet they not only became proper monks and followed a strict ascetic life, but some even managed to ascend to the peak of the theoretical life, to the vision of God (*theoptia*), and to see already from this life the glory of God, that is, the uncreated light. These illiterates became chosen vessels of grace and obtained gifts.

And all this, because they were assimilated by the spirit of the older fathers and they struggled following in their footsteps.

In the old times you would find elders with the prayer-rope in hand and a backpack on their back travelling long distances through the rugged trails. Their bodies were dried out by many years of ascetic struggle, their eyes were deep hollows from the vigils, and their mouth was parched from continually fasting till the ninth hour. Some old ascetics were recluses in their cells. They would not go to Karyes or to Daphne for provisions, but God would send angels of love, monks, who would help them. They had not human consolations and worldly comforts, but they themselves felt self-sufficient, without needs, and were completely free of cares. Other reverend elders, who lived patiently in a cenobium and were whitened in obedience and in the obediences, breathed God and Elder and reached measures of dispassion.

Many old ascetics, dry from asceticism, concealed within them spirit and life. Externally they were unwashed with old, filthy, and torn robes, but in this unkempt vessel they were hiding the precious treasures, the divine grace which they acquired by so great contests and day-and-nightly struggles. They were strangers to the world but familiars of God. They were ignorant of worldly developments but knew well "the way that leadeth unto life everlasting." They endured hardships and prayed for them that live in luxury and ease. They kept vigil for them that sleep. They shed tears and repented for them that laugh. Although far removed from the world, they felt all men as their brothers and embraced them all in their prayer.

The old fathers had simplicity in their way of life but also in their character. They did not consider themselves spiritual. They had knowledge of their weaknesses and lived in repentance. They wished to each other "a good repentance and a good end."

You cannot easily find these sanctified elders which exist up to this day, because they know how to hide themselves artfully. But even if you were to meet them you must have spiritual sensors to be able to recognise them and to communicate with them. Many fathers did not reveal their experiences nor their Godly-wise teaching. They took them with themselves as a mystical offering to the Lord who sets the contests. Others, however, wishing to help younger monks, would give advice or reveal some of their experiences, while other things were allowed by God's *economia* to be perceived by a third person. These known achievements of theirs become occasions for ascetic struggles for the youngers, tangible examples of the presence of God and refutation of those who delegate them to the past. Each generation has its own God-pleasing present which then becomes past.

Thorns and weeds have never been absent from the Garden of the the Panagia, but in older times there were many virtuous strugglers in the cenobia, in the desert, and even in the idiorrhythmic monasteries. Thus there was good encouragement for spiritual things. Discussions were always about miracles, ascetic feats, and salvation. The Holy Mountain at that time was far from the world, more hesychastic, more secret, quieter, more ascetical. The old Athonites especially had more respect for Tradition, for the principles, and for the institutions. They respectfully kept whatever they received from their predecessors. They had great reverence for the Panagia and trust in her providence. They were patient in illnesses, in temptations, and in trials, and they would not forget the purpose of their renunciation, the salvation of their soul. They were real pilgrims; their life was woven together with labour. They were deprived of material goods and avoided comfort. They had simplicity and not rationalism, experiences and not barren knowledge; they had a monk's ethos.

So from these men that do violence[3] to their nature and desire the Kingdom of the heavens, by coming to know their persistent and variform ascetic struggles, their watchful (*neptic*) ascents, their simple and unadulterated ethos, and their total giving of themselves to God,

---

3   See Mt. 11:12: "the kingdom Heaven suffereth violence, and the violent take it by force." The difference between this violence and the one of which worldly men speak, which makes this one necessary for salvation and that one conducive to damnation, is that this violence is exercised upon oneself for to fulfil the commandments of Christ, while that one is exercised upon others for selfish and ungodly ends. —ED.

we, too, can receive incorruptible fire that our zeal may be ignited unto struggles and prayer.

It is our honour that the grace of God has enrolled us in the monastic order and that we belong to the great Athonite family. It is our debt and duty to respect the Athonite monastic tradition, to follow in the footsteps of the older fathers, to attempt to live as they lived and to do their deeds.

All the things that are mentioned in this present book are deeds (ascetical feats or falls) and practical teaching of Athonites. They are written down so as to move us to repentance and imitation of their ascetical way of life or to make us cautious by their stumblings.

Morphologically this book has been divided into the following parts:

A. *Synaxaria (Lives of the Saints)*. We refer to the lives, the ascetical achievements, the divine assistance, and the teaching of elders about whom enough material has been found for the composition of a summary synaxarion.

B. *Incidents.* This unit records miracles, appearances of saints or demons, falls or delusions of some monks with the purpose of instruction. The names of those deluded are intentionally omitted.

C. *Apophthegms (Sayings)*. We mention elders in alphabetical order with brief instruction and ascetic struggles in a condensed, apophthegmatic form. Many of them are well-known, while some of them have books written about them, but all apophthegms herein mentioned are unknown and unpublished. The apophthegms are short but very potent because they come from the practice and struggles of Athonites and express the old spirit. Perhaps in some of these apophthegms there might appear to be some contradiction; e.g. one recommends saying the Jesus prayer during services, while another recommends paying attention to the hymns. The fathers speak simply, from their own experience, how they themselves were helped and not dogmatically.

D. *Sayings and Narrations of Elder Païsius*. Elder Païsius narrates concerning some old monks whom he came to know and mentions various incidents. He himself speaks generaly about the spiritual life and especially the monastic life, expressing various counsels and apophthegms. Intensely evident is his respect for the Athonite tradition and his interest in its continuation, while his observations and counsels constitute useful aids for our monastic struggle. Because of the extensiveness of the material it is a separate unit.

E. *The spirit of the old Athonites.*

This can be seen in the other parts of this book as well, but in the fifth section it is emphasised through the various narrations of the fathers. Thus the difference of the spirit and way of life of the old Athonites from those of us moderns can be discerned. It is natural for the general arrogance and corruption of our age also to influence the contemporary monks who are its children. With the lack of men on the Holy Mountain before the millennial celebration a gap was created and the tradition was weakened. The Panagia arranged so that new living material arrived. Perhaps, however, the old spirit was not sufficiently assimilated. For this cause we see spiritual deficiencies. Perhaps our judgements today should be more clement. Maybe in the eyes of God the little that the young monks do counts as much. Yet it is indisputable that in the old days there were many virtuous, hallowed elders who kept monasticism and had a monk's mindset. Their ascetical struggles and their supernatural experiences evoke wonder. The views of reposed fathers are given with their names, while those of living fathers, anonymously. Nevertheless, all of them speak with respect and nostalgia for the old, authentic Athonite spirit.

Here some explanations are in order:

—While we do mention well-known fathers, we do not mention things published by others, as far as we are able to know. Only in the synaxaria, lest there be a gap, we have written some well-known incidents, e.g. the appearances of the Panagia to Papa-Andrew, the abbot of Saint Paul's, et alia.

—We mention apophthegms and contests of renowned fathers but also of fathers "not very exceptional in asceticism." Some who had come to know these fathers with their human imperfections might perhaps disbelieve or have some other estimation of them. These things are written to benefit and to move the readers to repentance and not to justify the fathers. "It is God that justifieth. Who is he that condemneth?" We are not trying to make saints of the fathers, for thus we would be degrading the saints. Some of them had deficiencies, but we emphasise their contests and their virtues for our benefit. They were bearers of the old monastic spirit of the Athonite tradition. The things written down are few and only representative, due to the lack of preserved information.

—We emphasise the value of the Athonite tradition and bring out of its treasure things new and old. We mention fathers that lived longer ago but also contemporary ones (anonymously) who are still alive, since the tradition is living yet without judging the present situation.

The pieces of information were collected with much labour and attention, either from immediate observation and personal hearing or from the narrations of other elders about older ones, and, once they were checked, they were recorded as much as possible simply, honestly, and without exaggerations.

Infinite thanks are owed to all those who entrusted us with various pieces of information (and they are many), and to all the others who helped this present publication in secret, in whatever way.

May the fathers herein mentioned forgive me for daring to publish their achievements. They no longer have need of praises and acclaim, but for us these things are instructive and salvific, because they are our models and our guides.

May the good God also forgive me because, although I came to know virtuous elders, yet not having healthy spiritual sensors I did not understand the divine grace that they hid inside of them, with the result that I was not benefitted. Due to my pride I underestimated them and contemned them, judging from the externals. Let the readers at least be benefited, and let them pray for the unmonkish monk that laboured, who only sings the praises of the Athonite fathers and unfortunately does not imitate them.

View of Athos from Lakkoskiti

The shelter "Panagia" as seen from the peak

Father Gregory the Confessor

Father George the Confessor was born in the historic town of Messolonghi and was a child at the time of the heroic Exodus from Messolonghi in April 1826. His surname was Manolatos, indicating that his family probably descended from the island of Kefalonia. As an adult, he became a monk and priest in New Skete, residing in the monastic cell of Saint Spyridon. Due to his exceeding virtue, the fathers of New Skete recommended he be transferred to the presiding monastery of Saint Paul, where he became a spiritual father. During these years he also resided in the monastic cell of Saint John the Forerunner in the community of Saint Anne.

In about the middle of the 1840s he moved to the community of Little Saint Anne in order to strive for a deeper spiritual life, and he decided to live in the cell of the Dormition of the Theotokos. His small circle of followers consisted of the hieromonks Father Kosmas and Father Damian.

Their kept their rule of daily prayer and services rigorously and celebrated the Divine Liturgy every day. On Sundays they prayed the vigil with the fathers from the neighboring communities, sometimes in one cell, and sometimes in another. The area in which the community of Little Saint Anne was located was very isolated, deserted, and barren. However, the zeal of the fathers for the ascetic life overcame all these difficulties. Father Gregory and his fellow monks made woven undershirts, woolen socks, and garters, and lived off what little money they made from selling them. They also planted a small garden, so that they could grow the necessary fruits and vegetables for their sustenance.

They lived a hesychastic and ascetic life, without busyness or distractions. The few visitors that made it all the way to their cell came to confess to Father Gregory, who already had a reputation for being a virtuous and discerning spiritual father with strict principles. He excelled in this role. He viewed the fellow monks who confessed to him through the prism of the ascetic ideal, and the reason he was strict was precisely because he sought this exactness and perfection. He had spiritual power and knowledge. He fasted so strictly that he would not permit himself any oil, not only on Wednesdays and Fridays, but also church feasts and Bright Week. As a person, he was meek, quiet, and imposing, but the joy of his soul always brightly radiated through him. He was not a scholar by any means, but through continuous study of the Scriptures and ascetic writings he acquired a wealth of spiritual knowledge.

He was very experienced, bringing every difficult situation to a suitable conclusion, providing appropriate spiritual medicine like an experienced physician. He even had a certain heightened spiritual discernment with respect to the thoughts and visions of the fathers.

There was a time when Father Daniel of the cell of the Holy Archangels visited Father Gregory for confession, sharing with him that he saw the three hierarchs in a vision. Immediately he rushed to venerate Saint Basil, but the "saint" extended his foot, telling him to venerate his big toe. When he heard this, Father Gregory with his spiritual insight discerned the delusion and told the monk: "You venerated a great devil, brother. If it were truly Saint Basil in your vision, he would never have told you to venerate his toe."

The hesychast Callinicus also confessed to Father Gregory. At one time the feast of his hesychastic community was drawing near, and he asked his spiritual father if he was allowed to serve oil at the meal, since the feast fell on a Wednesday. Father Gregory answered: "Ascetics always fast, whether or not it's a feast." Obeying these instructions, they celebrated the festal meal without oil.

Elder Callinicus had a disciple, and this disciple often went to Daphne[1] to retrieve his elder's correspondence. For this reason, he

---

1   The main port for the Holy Mountain. —TRANS.

frequently needed to do the prescribed church services with his prayer-rope while he was on the road. However, at one point he began to question whether his praying in this way really "counted" as a service. He confided this to their spiritual father, Father Gregory, who, in his practical way, asked the disciple:

"If you found a wallet on the road to Daphne, and you took it, would that count as theft?"

"Well, of course", he answered. "It would be a sin and I'd have to confess it."

"So, since this evil thing that you would have done on the road counts as evil and would harm your soul, the prayers that you do on that same road with the prayer-rope don't count? Of course they do, and you shouldn't let thoughts like this trouble you."

With this answer from his spiritual father the disciple was comforted and was no longer troubled by this temptation.

Another time, a notorious criminal, "*Kapetan* Georgakis," showed up at the Iviron monastery. He wanted to receive Holy Communion, threatening to burn down the monastery if the monks refused him. The fathers found themselves in an awkward dilemma and decided to call Father Gregory. With his placid manner and spiritual grace, the elder pacified the robber and then proceeded to counsel him. Georgakis listened to the father's advice, first confessing to him and fasting, and then later on receiving the Holy Gifts and completely changing his way of life.

Once, Father Gregory went to the market in Karyes[2] to sell his handiwork. He laid it out it in front of him, then lowered his monk's cap, and bending his head down started saying the Jesus Prayer. At that time, the exiled Patriarch Joachim III was passing by there. He saw the elder at the awning of the cemetery holding his prayer-rope with his gaze fixed downward. It made an impression on him, and he asked to learn who that monk was. Finding out it was the renowned spiritual father, Gregory, he was overjoyed and drew near, saying, "Father, do you not advertise your handiwork? You must look up if you want to find customers to whom to sell it."

2   The main town on Athos, at around the center of the peninsula.—TRANS.

Without raising his head to look at the Patriarch, the monk answered, "Your all-holiness, whoever has need of my handiwork can see it and can buy it. I do not need to seek out customers."

"I did not come to bother you, father. I just came to tell you that someday I will come visit you."

"Thank you, your all-holiness, but you do not need to make the effort, as my cell is very small, and the ceiling is low, so unfortunately it cannot fit a Patriarch."

"Never mind that. I will bend down and I will fit."

"Your eminence, if you were able to bend down, you would not be an exile here. You would be in your See in Constantinople", the monk answered, referring to the imperiousness and intransigence of this great Patriarch.

The Patriarch marveled at this laconic and apt response, and his acquaintance with Father Gregory became a landmark in his life. Indeed, he later visited Little Saint Anne frequently, and made Father Gregory his spiritual father. He would describe him as a pillar of virtue and a great exemplar of the monastic life. Since the monks in the community lacked many of the basics, the Patriarch also sent him liturgical vessels, ecclesiastical books, and different housewares: plates, glasses, cups, et cetera., so the other fathers in the area could borrow them for their feasts.

There was another instance when a certain bishop, who was invited to officiate at the feast of the Great Lavra, passed by Father Gregory's cell. Seeing an opportunity, he asked to go to confession with him. Father Gregory, discerning the bishop's soul with his spiritual insight, perceived that he had an impediment, and would not agree to confess him, explaining that the hierarch would not obey the penance he would impose. The bishop assured him that he would do whatever Father Gregory saw fit, and with that, he was allowed to confess. The spiritual father told him to resign from the episcopacy. The bishop accepted this, though concerned for what would happen with the feast of the Great Lavra that was coming up

The skull of Father Gregory

His cell, the "Dormition of the Theotokos".

in a few days. Father Gregory suggested he give up the omophorion[3] and become a schema-monk, which is what happened.

The anchorites were also in frequent contact with Father Gregory on account of his virtue. Blessed Elder Gabriel, abbot of the monastery of Dionysiou, preserved, and later shared, one such instance. Father Gregory was speaking to him, and said, "I was celebrating the Divine Liturgy on Holy Thursday, and towards the end of the service, a young monk appeared in the small church in my cell, holding a small lamp. He told me, 'You should not consume the Communion yet, holy father, as there are three monks who live close here who need to commune. This is why I came to fetch you.'

"I agreed, without further inquiry, and I followed him, holding the Holy Eucharist. After a little while, despite the steep ascent and my advanced age, we arrived at a spacious cave where three monks were waiting for us. They immediately partook of the Holy Gifts, and having thanked me, they asked imploringly: 'Holy father, can you also come to commune us on Holy Thursday next year? But please do not say anything to anyone about this and whatever you saw here.'

"Obviously, after all I saw and heard I did not ask any questions, and, following the youth, I descended on the path back. After a little while, he stopped to prostrate and venerate the holy tabernacle[4], and bade me walk ahead, telling me he would be along shortly. Once I had gone a little way, I turned to see if he was coming, but he was nowhere to be seen. The whole experience was extraordinary, but I abided by their request and did not say anything to anyone.

"But then this happened: in our Skete[5] it is customary for the fathers to gather together on the Saturday of Lazarus for the vigil of the Entrance of the Lord into Jerusalem. After the vigil, as we all gathered in the refectory for the usual refreshments, I heard someone say:

---

3   A bishop's distinguishing liturgical garment, designating him as a member of the episcopacy.—TRANS.

4   A container for the reserved Gifts (Gr. artophorion).—TRANS.

5   A monastic community, usually small, under the care of one of the larger, established Athonite monasteries.—TRANS.

"'How monasticism has declined in our day and age! There aren't any anchorites anymore, as there were in the old times!'

"Then, either from carelessness or by being carried away, I exclaimed:

"'But there are, by the grace of God! Even today they exist, by the grace of Christ!'

"And when they asked me where, I replied 'Over there on Aimon' (the smaller mountain on the foothills of Athos) and I indicated with my hand.

"My story made an impression on everyone, but they did not ask me more, as, tired from the all-night vigil and exhausted from the forty-day Lenten fast, they were ready to leave. I departed for my cell as well, regretting my revelation. During Divine Liturgy on Holy Thursday the next year, that young monk appeared again, and with a nod, told me the purpose of his visit. When I finished the liturgy, I took the Holy Eucharist and followed him, once again arriving at the cave. There, once they had all communed of the sacred Mysteries, the older of them turned to me and asked:

"'Why, holy father, did you ignore our request and reveal our presence to the brethren?'

"When I did not respond, he continued:

"'It doesn't matter, but on account of your indiscretion you should not come to commune us next year. If you do come, you shall find us as the all-good God desires, but we beseech you again, not to reveal our existence.'

"I left on my own, and could not have been more in awe about these strange men, and how they knew the things I said at the Skete. I finally concluded that they were holy men. The next year, I did not take the Holy Gifts but carried only antidoron and holy water. With much effort I ascended to the cave and found the three elders dead. The fourth was clearly an angel of the Lord that served them. They were on their backs on the ground in a peaceful position with their hands crossed on their chests, as if they were sleeping. I knelt, kissed their hands and foreheads, and concluded from the dryness of their holy relics that they had departed for the Eternal Mansions on the same Great and Holy Thursday that they had communed of the pure Mysteries."[6]

Another time, while Father Gregory was finishing the Divine Liturgy, before he had consumed the gifts, he saw seven ascetics in rags, who nevertheless shone with divine grace. A beam of light seemed to travel with them. Seeing him looking at them with surprise, they said: "Holy spiritual father, we know of your life. We live here, a little further up, and we are here to ask your permission to come to you so that you may commune us. Only we bind you that you should not tell anyone what you saw, because then you will not see us again."

Father Gregory accepted, and so for a time the seven naked invisible ascetics[7] were coming and he was communing them. On the day that he knew the invisible naked ascetics would come, he did not consume the holy mysteries, but waited for them while praying. They entered through the side door with modesty and holy propriety, with a silent and humble step, one behind the other, radiant with the grace of the ascetic life, and with piety and contrition they communed of the pure Body and Blood of the Lord. They were always silent, and with slight bows they asked forgiveness and thanked the spiritual father as he communed them. He kept the secret well and rejoiced that he was serving these sanctified monks.

One day, however, a young monk came to confess to him. He was overwhelmed by temptations, disappointed, and ready to leave the monastery and return to the world, saying that true virtue no longer existed on the Holy Mountain. The spiritual father tried to dissuade him, telling him that these thoughts came from the evil one, that virtue does exist, and that it is hidden and is not apparent. The young monk, however, was not convinced, asking for a tangible

---

6   Από τον κήπο τού παππού, ἔκδ. το Περιβόλι τῆς Παναγίας, 1994, σελ. 71-74.

7   Accordance to the living and many times confirmed Athonite tradition there are seven, or according to others twelve, monks, who live on Athos the most perfect ascetic life and are praying constantly for the whole world. When one of them dies, another takes his place and the number remains stable. They are also sometimes called 'naked', because they wear old cassocks. They have the grace of invisibility. When they desire, they become invisible to men.

example. Then, in order to save a soul, the spiritual father revealed the hidden mystery. When the day that the seven ascetics came to commune arrived, he put the youth in a cell across from the church so that he might see while remaining hidden. The seven came as usual and communed, but before leaving, the last said to him, "Holy father, we thank you for communing us for so many years, but since you broke our agreement and revealed our secret, you will not see us again."

The previously tempted young monk was shaken by what he saw, and with tears and contrition he asked for forgiveness, having decided to stay on the Holy Mountain and to struggle for the salvation of his soul.

The spiritual father sadly nodded and said to him, "You were saved, but I, for your sake, have lost a most valuable treasure."

From then on Father Gregory fell into deep sorrow due to the loss of contact with those holy, equal-to-the-angels, naked, and invisible anchorites, and being already advanced in age he fell asleep in the Lord in the year 1899, faithful to his monastic struggle until his death in his ninetieth year.

Before his passing, he told the brotherhood every detail about the naked and invisible ascetics, for their benefit and example and to the glory of God.

When they transferred the renowned spiritual father's bones[8], his skull had the color of holy relics and many smelled a fragrant odor.

May we have his blessing. Amen.

---

8   Per the custom on Athos, the reposed monk is buried only for a time, then later his bones are removed from the ground and cleaned to be placed in the ossuary. At this time is when monks often discover if any reposed monk has possessed the grace of incorruption.—TRANS.

Father Daniel the Hesychast

Father Daniel of the cell of Saint Peter the Athonite was a great hesychast in his generation and an imitator of Saint Peter the Athonite, the first and greatest of Athonite hesychasts. He lived his ascetic struggle in the same place, but due to his way of life and the chronology, very few elements from his ascetic lifestyle have come down to us.

His place of origin and his life in general before he became a monk are not known. He became a monk at the cell of Saint Peter, and was tonsured by a virtuous elder and spiritual father, Anthony[1], who later became elder of the cave and veneration site on September 15th, 1874. Since he excelled both at obedience and in the monastic struggle, Father Daniel was judged by his elder worthy to receive the grace of the priesthood. He was ordained at the Lavra a deacon and then a priest, and from then on did not leave the hesychastic dwelling of Saint Peter's, never venturing out until his death.

On April 1st, 1909 he was acknowledged as an elder[2] and spiritual father, his own elder having apparently lived until that date.

Elder Daniel had the discipline of keeping vigil all night. He considered it a sin to be found in bed while it was dark. He rested in the afternoon, and when night fell he began his daily vigil. At the end of the vigil every day he would celebrate the Divine Liturgy or, during Great Lent, the Presanctified Liturgy. His Divine Liturgies would last for hours, as he was often lost in the Divine Vision, and

---

1   Bishop Chrysostom of Rodostolos, *Πόθος καί χάρις στόν Ἄθωνα*, Mt. Athos 2000, pg. 221.
2   Ibid. pg. 222.

on account of his great awe and spiritual fervor, he had difficulty saying the litanies.

In the morning he rested a little, and during the day, wearing a cassock and *koukoulion*,[3] he did whatever jobs were necessary around his cell, or he confessed monks. It was apparent to those who saw him that during the whole day he did not interrupt his spiritual work, and he avoided unnecessarily communicating and speaking with others.

At noon he would eat his meager meal and withdraw to rest for his nightly vigil. His life was ascetic and simple. He did not even have windowpanes in the windows. He had one fireplace and some old built-in chimneys in a place that got over two meters of snow in the winter.

One time an elder sent a monk under him to confess to Father Daniel. The monk went, knocked on the door saying, "Through the prayers..."[4], but did not receive a response. He looked in through the window of the church and saw Father Daniel kneeling under the oil lamp which hung in front of his icons, praying and completely on fire. Running back to his elder in a panic, he told him that Father Daniel was burning to death. They raced back to Saint Peter's together and found Father Daniel peaceful and in a normal state.

Father Daniel eventually took on a disciple, tonsuring him and naming him Anthony after his own elder. There was a time when the disciple fell ill and had to go to the Lavra where he remained until he recovered. During that period a neighbor of Father Daniel who lived in a neighboring cell a little further down came daily and chanted the liturgy with him. Father Daniel would do the *kairos*[5] and

---

3   A broad hood worn over the *skoupho* (the monastic cap) that falls onto the back of the wearer, the koukoulion is only worn in the divine services or in other formal settings, usually not at work. —TRANS.

4   It is the practice of monks, when knocking on the door of a room, to call out, "Through the prayers of our Holy Fathers," with a response of "Lord Jesus Christ, our God, have mercy on us" from inside. —TRANS.

5   The initial prayers that clergymen perform to start their preparation for the Divine Liturgy. —TRANS.

The cell of Saint Peter the Athonite (above, from the distance; below up close)

begin the *proskomidi*.[6] At the arranged time, the monk would come and they would begin the Divine Liturgy.

One day, Father Daniel had completed the proskomidi, but the monk who chanted the service for him had not shown up. Understanding that something must have happened to him, the holy father began to pray in sadness, not knowing what to do. At that moment he saw three monks entering. Without saying a word, they venerated, and began chanting the Divine Liturgy, which Father Daniel joyously celebrated.

When they finished, Father Daniel asked them who they were and how they found themselves in the desert at such an hour. They answered that they were the founders of the Monastery of Iveron and that the Lord had sent them. As soon as they had uttered those words, they disappeared.[7]

The grace-filled priest of the Highest, aside from his other gifts, had also communed the naked and invisible ascetics that were living and moving about in those places.

Elder Joseph the Hesychast, with his co-ascetic Elder Arsenius, would trek three hours through the night to attend liturgy and commune with Father Daniel. Elder Joseph noted that from as many ascetics as he knew—and at that time the desert was full of virtuous ascetics—Father Daniel had reached the highest condition of holiness.

"There was also another even more admirable elder at the cave of St. Peter the Athonite, Father Daniel, an imitator of St. Arsenios the Great. A profoundly silent recluse. He served Liturgy daily until the end of his life. For sixty years he never even thought of omitting the Divine Liturgy. Even during Great Lent, he served Presanctified Liturgies every day. He died in deep old age without ever getting sick. His Liturgy always lasted three and a half or four hours, because he couldn't say the petitions due to his compunction. He always soaked the ground in front of him with his tears. That is why he didn't want any strangers to be present at his Liturgy, so that they wouldn't see his

---

6   A service performed by the priest in the sanctuary that prepares the prosphora (loaves) for use in the Divine Liturgy. —TRANS.

7   Bishop Chrysostom of Rodostolos, *Πόθος καί χάρις στόν Ἄθωνα*, Mt. Athos 2000, ibid. pg. 222-224

work. But as for me, since I begged him very fervently, he accepted me. And every time I went--after walking three hours at night to attend that truly fearsome and divine spectacle--he told me one or two sayings as he left the altar and immediately hid himself until the next day. He had noetic prayer and all-night vigils throughout his life. It was from him that I also received my schedule and found great benefit. He ate only one hundred grams of bread every day. He was all rapt in his Liturgy; he never finished a Liturgy without the ground turning into mud from his tears."[8]

Out of gratitude for the great spiritual benefits they received from Father Daniel, Elder Joseph and Elder Arsenius would occasionally do some odd jobs for him, like building a small garden bed.

Aside from his disciple, Father Anthony, Father Daniel's monastic community included Father Peter, known as 'Petrakis,' or "little Peter," who imitated his mentor in his hesychastic way of life, and Father Gideon who was an educated man, and later ordained a priest.

When Father Daniel noticed that his disciple, Father Anthony, desired to be liked by men and tried to appear as a good disciple in front of others so that they would admire him, he decided to humble him; so, every time he would call him in public, he would say "Tony! Hey, Tony!"

When Father Daniel saw a plane flying for the first time, he said with bewilderment, "What is that? The world will be lost."

When the days of his life were fulfilled, and he perceived that he was approaching his end, Father Daniel, wearing his cassock, took a little walk about the yard of his cell, and looking to heaven, he turned his gaze about and cried out, "Vanity of vanities, all is vanity."

The same day, after celebrating the Divine Liturgy, he departed for eternal life peacefully, without sickness, full of days, and heavily laden with virtues and divine grace. The year was 1929.

May we have his blessing. Amen.

---

8   Elder Joseph, Monastic Wisdom, Florence 1998, p. 86-87.

The Possessionless Philaret of Karoulia

Elder Philaret of Karoulia was born in 1889 in Rysion in Constantinople. His parents were Apostolos and Maria Basmatsidi, and when he was baptized he was given the name Photios. He seems to have been raised with good principles, and his parents educated him comparatively well for the time. He felt a desire for the monastic life, so on August 17th, 1908, at the age of nineteen, he left his parents and country and moved to the monastery of Stavronikita on Mount Athos. The very next year he was tonsured a monk and given the name Philemon by the hierodeacon Jeremiah. On August 10th, 1918, he was tonsured to the great schema by Elder Cyril the blind, and his name was once again changed, this time to Philaret. On March 8th, 1919, he became the *proistamenos*[1] of the monastery. Before all this, however, in the beginning of his monastic life, he was given the position of sacristan[2] and when he was alone in his cell he struggled greatly towards the Kingdom. He wanted to live in the desert as an ascetic hermit and he found the idiorhythmic life[3] as a suitable preparatory environment.

Father Chrysostom, an old monk from the monastery of Stavronikita, explained that when he first joined the community, Elder Philaret surrounded him with his love. He even received him into

---

1 In monasteries, the monk first after the abbot in rank. —TRANS.

2 The monk in charge of keeping the church clean, preparing the church for services, and performing certain parts of the service that involve lighting candles and leading the liturgical entrances. —TRANS.

3 A monastic lifestyle where the monks live alone as opposed to cenobitic monasticism where monks live communally. —TRANS.

his cell and cooked for him. He made beans for two in the small *briki* [a kind of coffee pot], which he also used to make coffee. Over this meager meal, Elder Philaret provided the young monk with the advice and guidance about the monastic life which he had acquired from his valuable experience.

When Father Chrysostom was given the task of assistant to the sacristan, a certain *proistamenos* gave him a container with fifteen pounds of oil [for the lamps that hang before the icons] and told him to make it last, as he would not give him any more oil until the next year. Naturally this was impossible. In a state of bewilderment, Father Chrysostom asked for help from Elder Philaret, who told him that it was, indeed, possible for the oil to last. With quiet certainty, he explained, "When you fill the small oil container, go in front of the icon of the Panagia, make the sign of the cross over it, and ask her to bless it." Following his advice, Father Chrysostom always performed this prayer before filling the votive lamps, and through her miraculous intervention the minuscule amount not only lasted the year but there was even some left over.

Father Chrysostom also shared that the elder had told him, if he should see a storm at sea and some boat was in danger, to take the oil lamp from the icon of Saint Nicholas and spill it into the sea in order to calm it. Once, during Holy Week, Father Chrysostom went out to see if the nets that they had put along the coast had caught any fish. (Stavronikita was the poorest monastery, so they were not able to afford eggs, cheese, and fish for the feast of Pascha. Every monk was responsible for his own nourishment.) As he was there, he saw that the sea was turbulent, and one small boat was battling with the waves. Father Chrysostom remembered what Elder Philaret had said, so he immediately ran back, took the oil lamp of Saint Nicholas, and ran to the dock. He tried to throw the oil into the sea, but there was a strong wind and only a few drops fell into the water. In a few moments, however, the wind stopped and the sea was calm. The boat went on to the monastery of Vatopedi, unloaded fish, eggs, and cheese, and then returned to the dock of Stavronikita. They called the fathers and asked them to which saint the monastery was dedicated. When they heard that is was Saint

Elder Philaret of Karoulia

Nicholas, the patron saint of sailors and those at sea, they donated large amounts of what they had as a blessing for Pascha and to show their gratitude for the saint who had saved them.

Elder Philaret was diligent in his monastic duties, loved the services, and performed fasts, vigils, and prayers in his cell without the other fathers knowing. Since he knew that the base of spiritual life is humility, occasionally he would act as a fool for Christ, on the one hand, so that they might hold him in contempt and humble him, and on the other, so that he might retire from the position of *proistamenos* and depart for the hesychastic life in the desert.

Some of the things Elder Philaret would do when he was acting as a fool for Christ included leaving the monastery without a blessing[4] making disorderly movements not proper for a monk, and making a show of the monastery and the monastic schema. When he was asked about these actions, he told the Synaxis[5]: "I left from the monastery secretly and intentionally and traveled to Thasos[6] in order that I may be condemned as disobedient and unreasonable and be relieved from the position of *proistamenos*. I wish to remain in the monastery as a simple monk, so I will freely declare that I am resigning from this position voluntarily and without pressure on account of my weakness and ineptitude, and from this day the monastery can use me as a simple monk and appoint me to whichever service it wish" (Synaxis Meeting, October 1st, 1920). Then he placed his signature of the letter of resignation on Jan. 12th, 1921, and was given the duty of cellarer.

Elder Philaret used to tell Father Chrysostom: "I was waiting for you so that I could leave." He left him as his replacement and departed for the desert on March 12th, 1921. For a while he lived near the seashore of Saint Anne's and later went to Karoulia, which was down the mountain by the sea. His cell had a tiny church, only two meters wide, and when he was able to find a priest, they celebrated the Divine Liturgy.

---

4   I.e. permission. —TRANS.
5   An assembly of the monastic fathers. —TRANS.
6   An island immediately northeast of Athos. —TRANS.

He was completely possessionles. He did not want to keep supplies for more than a single day on hand, "because I could die tomorrow." He never wore shoes. Some people would give him a pair of shoes, he would wear them for a day, and then give them away. His cassocks were always clean, though old, frayed, and full of patches.

He also had a single cup and he would tell people that with it he was able to do three different jobs: drink water, use it for a spoon when he was cooking, and use it as a trowel when he built something. He was possessionless, extremely poor, ragged and shoeless, but from his great love he would sacrifice his peaceful existence and go to the neighboring cells to gather alms of whatever they wished to give. Then he would go around to the elders who were elderly and disabled and give to them.

He did not do handiwork: he was occupied with noetic prayer. He did not have a prayer-rope, but rather said the Jesus prayer moving his thumb as though he were holding a prayer-rope. He performed all the services by doing the Jesus prayer, and the only book he owned was the writings of abba Isaac whom he held as his teacher and guide.

Sometimes, in order to find complete stillness, he would seek refuge in the clefts of rocks, praying there for hours and days. During such times the demons would wage war, appearing in front of him, but he always drove them away with the sign of the cross saying, "Let God arise and let His enemies be scattered..." Other times they would throw stones on the tin roof of his cell, making a great noise, but the roof was never damaged.

He was a man of utter simplicity and a perfect sense of other-worldliness. He did not know if there were other men in the world, nor did he ask. He knew no one but other monks. He believed that in the end, only he and God existed in the world. He did long fasts, usually eating prickly pears and rusks. He would boil wild celery and eat nothing but that for a week. When his spiritual father would go commune him, he always left quickly, as he could not bear the foul odor from the rotten greens which Elder Philaret ate. Elder Gideon, who at the time was only a young monk, later said that

Elder Philaret advised him: "Eat greens like this, my child, and in the end the only other thing you will need to eat in order to live are a few rusks".

And while he was living so ascetically, there was a period during which Elder Philaret could not receive Holy Communion. He had confessed to his spiritual father that the day before he had eaten grouper, and since the monastic rules prohibited eating fish the day before Holy Communion, the spiritual father did not allow him to commune. Hearing this, another discerning elder perceived that something must have happened and questioned Elder Philaret in order to get to the bottom of it. It turned out that Elder Philaret referred to his wormy rusks as "grouper," not knowing that grouper was a fish. He had heard someone refer to his maggoty rusks in this way as a joke, but not understanding it and believing that is what they were called, he said that he ate grouper.

He was so spiritually sensitive and would make such a clean and thorough confession that even after many years had passed he remembered and confessed that when he was gardener at Stavroni-kita Monastery he harvested the squash when they were young and did not let them grow. He considered this unjust, and with deep repentance he would weep inconsolably.

During that period there was an elder at Saint Peter's that went and worked as a picker during hazelnut season. He asked Elder Philaret if he would be willing to live in and watch his cell during his absence. The elder acquiesced and went to live there. He stayed for two or three months, but he was not at peace and returned to Karoulia. Upon his return, however, the monk from Saint Peter's asked him for rent for the months that he lived there, despite the fact that he had previously never said anything about rent. Elder Philaret, being completely possessionless, had nothing with which to pay, and for this reason he worried, believing that he was to blame. From that point on, whenever he met someone on the road, he would bow his head saying, "Your blessing. Forgive me. I have wasted all my years of monastic labors, as I do not pay the rents that I owe." When the other fathers learned of this, they rebuked the monk that was seeking rent from the possessionless elder, and he immediately stopped troubling the blameless and wondrous elder.

He had genuine repentance and self-accusation. He was extremely placid and never became angry against anyone. He had once visited the cell of Elder Gerontius from the community of the Danielites. As usual, he was barefoot. Gerontius rebuked him sharply in front of the all the guests, pilgrims, and other young monks, saying: "Don't ever come barefoot again. At least wear slippers. You're a hypocrite, pretending to be holy." Philaret accepted the rebukes completely undisturbed and made a bow while repeating: "Please forgive me."

The next day when he went to the Danielites, he wore the slippers that he kept outside his cell, and they marveled at his humility. Elder Gerontius then explained to him that he did what he had done the previous day in order to teach the young monks about self-accusation and humility, but that the elder could and should walk however he wishes.

During church feasts, the monks of Karoulia would gather together in a hut with a small built-in church, read the service, chant the Paraklesis, and when they did not have a priest they would also read the Gospel. They had Elder Philaret do it, as he was educated, and intoned it like the priests. Another elder reprimanded him, telling him he should not be chanting or intoning, as he is not a priest, to which Elder Philaret replied, "Forgive me." The next time he read the Gospel, however, he was carried away by his fervor and read it melodically. He did not do this for show, but from simplicity and a pious disposition, as a psalmodic offering. At the meal after the service they once again rebuked him, this time publicly. He made a bow to every one of them, saying: "Bless me, fathers, I have wasted the years of my monastic labors. Again I read melodically."

When the brotherhood of Elder Gerasimus the hymnographer began building the church in the cave of the holy fathers, some fathers of the Skete, fearing that they may not be able to finish it, were saying that it was better they not start. The monks, hearing these things, were saddened. One day, Elder Philaret came to visit and told them, "Brothers, this work is pleasing to God. I saw Saint

Dionysius above the cave, blessing it. He told me that he himself would protect the church of the cave, and it will be preserved until the end of time." From that day he began visiting the cave at night to pray.

At the end of his life, Elder Philaret was sick for a month. His stomach hurt and he would not eat. He foresaw his end and prepared, bidding farewell to his neighbors and asking and receiving forgiveness from them. And so, on his own, without anyone by his side, he gave up his spirit into the hands of the living God in 1956, at the age of 67. The fathers found him asleep in the Lord with his hands crossed, and they buried him in the tomb that he had prepared. In his cell they found only a washboard with which he cleaned his clothes in the sea, a blanket, and the book of Saint Isaac the Syrian. His neighbor, Elder Gabriel of Karoulia, guarded his relics along with the relics of Elder Seraphim in a cave after their transfer. His skull is entirely yellow.[7]

May we have his blessing. Amen.

---

7   In the Athonite experience, when a monk's skull is discovered to be yellow, this is a confirmation from God of the monastic's righteous and saintly life. —TRANS.

'Little Peter' the Hesychast

George Lagios, as he was known in the world,[1] was born on the island of Lemnos in the year 1891. It seems that when he was young he was not helped spiritually, and for this reason he would drink and get drunk. These things are written down here just as they have been preserved by his old acquaintances, so that some of his unusual monastic and ascetic practices can be explained and understood.

The good God, seeing his good disposition, granted the flame of repentance to this simple and rare soul and in 1908 he arrived at Mount Athos to become a monk.

His desire for hesychasm and the fame of the great hesychast, Father Daniel of the cell of Saint Peter, led his steps to the most isolated and hesychastic area, to the cell in which Saint Peter the Athonite, the first and greatest of Athonite hesychasts, lived ascetically. He became Father Daniel's disciple and tried to imitate his struggles and be fully obedient to him.

After a prolonged novitiate he became a monk in the year 1926 with the name of Peter. He learned the practice of monastic life from his sanctified elder and through him was initiated into the mysteries of hesychia, watchfulness, the cloistered life, and unceasing noetic prayer, all of which he kept until his death.

Living in a state of deep repentance for the sins of his youth, both in knowledge and in ignorance, he asked for and received a blessing from his elder to abstain from water for three months, so

---

1   I.e. before he became a monk. —TRANS.

that God may forgive the excessive imbibing of his youth. He ate food and greens, of course, but he did not drink water for three months.

He was both eager and courageous in his ascetic struggles and with the great simplicity that characterized him he was perfectly obedient to his elder. This good start and the spiritual foundation which it laid was a preface to his later glorious path.

When Father Daniel fell asleep in the Lord, around the year 1929, Peter lived with some neighboring monks for a few years. One of them left the community and went out into the world. The others passed away and it seems he found it difficult to live alone. The brutal years of the Occupation and starvation came,[2] and in 1940 he was forced to leave his cell of repentance and move to a small dry hut near Little Saint Anne's, beyond the hut of Saint Thomas the Apostle, below the road which leads to Katounakia. It is not easily found, as it is inside a mountain boulder. He had two small cells with low ceilings. An exterior door led to the boulder, where there is a rather spacious cave with an opening for light. Here the elder isolated himself in order to find stillness.

This was his spiritual workshop, his spiritual hive, "his sweet Katouni[3]." It was paradise on earth for him, as here he could taste the honey of silence and the manna of heaven. For this reason he did not have the heart to leave his hut to socialize and converse with others. This small-framed, illiterate, and poor 'little Peter' was a hesychast of the highest caliber. He had mastered unceasing prayer, he often saw the Uncreated Light, and even during his earthly life he lived in a paradisal state.

Elder Gerasimus the Hymnographer explained; "I met Elder Peter (little Peter) of Katounakia. He was indeed a holy monk. He prayed much and was extremely ascetic. He cooked once a week and ate from that same food every day. Once he came to our cell transformed in appearance. Weeping, he told me that the night

---

2   Sc. during World War Two, when Greece was occupied by German, Italian, and Bulgarian forces. —ED.

3   A small pedestrian alley, path, or *cul de sac*, often paved with cobblestones, found in older Mediterranean villages and towns. —TRANS.

before while he was praying he was surrounded by an all-encompassing white light, and his cell was filled with a sweet scent. He felt an indescribable blessedness, sweetness, and peace, and did not know if he was in his cell or in heaven. He wanted to know what had happened to him, asking me, 'You are educated and know how to read: can you tell me if this is a Satanic deception? Is it something evil?' Everything he had told me was clearly a sign of grace, and as he was describing these things he was beside himself, and for one instant his face suddenly shone and I was stunned. I was not speaking, letting him continue without interruption. I was imprinting everything he was saying in my own memory. I reviewed all he said, and discerned no sign of delusion. I later told him to glorify God, as he was found worthy to see these things, because all of it was from God and not satanic delusions. As he was leaving he implored me not to discuss this with anyone, and to beseech God to have mercy on him so that he not become deluded. Elder Peter was a man of noetic prayer, a very humble and simple monk."

It seems that this was the first time any such thing had happened to him, but from that time on and thereafter he experienced many such events, as he later revealed to Saint Païsius. He often saw the Uncreated Light, and had the grace of an unceasing flow of tears which accompanied his unceasing prayer, having transcended the monastic typica.[4]

A certain elder asked him if he had a set prayer rule and service schedule, to which he answered, "I have neither. As soon as the sun sets I eat, do the Compline service, and sleep for two hours. When I wake up it is night, and I begin praying with the prayer-rope. By the second or third prayer-rope the tears come, and until the morning I do not know where I am. During the summer I begin the vigil in the evening, and when the sun comes out I usually come to my senses and go inside." (He was most likely caught up in *theoria*.)

It was for this reason that he lived a cloistered life and did not want to converse. "he does not wish to be hindered from partaking of the sweetness of God."[5] He avoided socializing precisely because he

4   The prescribed life a monk is expected to live. —TRANS.
5   *The Ladder of Divine Ascent*, 27:27

The hut of Elder Peter

did not want to lose his constant connection to God. "He who loves conversing with Christ loves to become a monastic."[6] Other fathers would visit him and knock on the outside door, but he, opening the window a crack, would ask who it was and what he wanted. If they had brought him food, he would tell them to leave it outside, and he would not go out to get it until it had rotted. He did this so that the fathers would see the rotten food and not bring him any more.

Someone asked him why he did not come out of his cell, to which he answered, "If I were to come out, we would just engage in superfluous words." He lived without possessions. One or two times a year he would come out in order to trade his handiwork, prayer-ropes, for bread rusks. He fasted until the ninth hour every day and almost wholly abstained from oil. His usual meal was tea with rusks. He also did three-day fasts on a regular basis.

---

6   St. Isaac the Syrian, *Ascetic Homilies*, Homily 34, 152.

When Father Dionysius of Little Saint Anne's was still a young monk, Elder Peter had told him: "In order to live in the desert, you must be a good cook. You will cook beans on Sunday and eat them till Tuesday. On Wednesday you'll throw in a little water and boil some more beans, on Thursday you'll add a bit of tomato, on Friday a little salt and water, on Saturday you'll also put in a little flour gruel, and on Sunday you can cook another dish. In this way you can go a whole week with a single dish."

There was a time when it had snowed, and Father Dionysios, who lived in the cell across the way, saw Father Peter going to and fro barefoot in the snow. Asking him why he was doing that, the elder revealed that he was struggling with carnal thoughts, and he fought them by going barefoot in the snow.

Elder Peter had the grace of seeing things that would happen in the future. One day he received a revelation and went to the elder who at the time lived in the cell of Saint Haralambos in New Skete to warn him, "Father, did you know that a wolf is coming to devour your little sheep? Your disciple is not doing well. Be careful because he will throw away the monastic schema and leave." And truly, the monk was consumed by temptations and planning to leave. Elder Peter saw it from Little Saint Anne's, but unfortunately, despite the effort of his elder, he left the monastic life and got married.

He lived completely without distractions. During summer he would climb up Mount Athos, supposedly to gather tea, but in reality he was practicing stillness and giving himself over to noetic and unceasing prayer and contemplation. He did not have many contacts and tried to live unnoticed, and for this reason there is not much information that has been preserved about his life. As the Holy Fathers note, however, many times a single word is sufficient to reveal the entire spiritual state and internal workings of a monk. If someone tries a small glass of wine he knows the quality of the whole barrel. And from the information that we do have, it seems that Elder Peter was advanced in prayer, a monk of prayer, secret work, who "took the kingdom of God by force," a true ascetic, in whom contemplation and action were inextricably joined.

All the fathers who knew him spoke of him in glowing terms: "He was the best monk in the area," "A true monk," "A most holy little elder." Saint Païsius also noted that of all the ascetics he knew, Elder Peter had reached the highest level of holiness, and for that reason he wanted to become his disciple.

Father Ephraim of Katounakia greatly respected Elder Peter and told others, "When you met that man and he spoke to you, he left you with a certain sweetness inside your soul. He never came to vigils and he never caused a scandal. Living on the Holy Mountain for a lifetime and retaining your peace with all is a great accomplishment."

When Elder Peter met other monks on the road he did not greet them with the customary "your blessing", but with the following profound saying: "Brothers, we are departing" (that is, we are dying).

He had great tact. He avoided spending the night in other monks' cells, mostly so that he would not be a burden to them, but also lest he lose his own inner peace and break his prayer rule. There was a time when Elder Joachim of the cell of the Ascension in Karyes (which belongs to Vatopedi) was pressing him to stay the night, but he did not accept. He headed for Daphne by foot. As he walked, darkness fell and it began to rain. He spent the night in the hollow of a chestnut tree.

When he perceived that his death was approaching, he left his cell at Little Saint Anne's and went to the place where he had begun his monastic life and found repentance, Saint Peter's. He desired to leave his earthy remains in that place. He lived there for a few months and fell asleep in the Lord in the year 1958, on the feast-day of Saint Peter the Athonite, whose name he had taken and to whose name the church of his cell was dedicated. When he passed away, the only things that were found in his cell were a few rusks in a wicker basket and half a bottle of oil for the votive lamp. He had neither a bed nor a mattress.

May we have his blessing. Amen.

The Ascetic Gabriel of Karoulia

Elder Gabriel, the great ascetic of Karoulia, was born in the year 1903 in the village of Platani, in Achaea. His father's name was Demetris Voyatzoglou, and his mother's Pagona. They baptized him George.

When George was still an infant in his mother's arms, she was rocking him saying, "When my baby grows up, I'll give him the best wedding." The infant answered, "I'll become a monk." "Knock on wood!" she replied.

When he came of age, he became a policeman and served in Kalamata.

When he finally decided to become a monk, his sister saw a dream that he was leaving for the monastery while she showered him with flowers. He asked her: "Do you really want me to be a monk?" To which she answered: "Is there anything better?" Every time her parents remembered this story they were greatly saddened, as she had known that he was leaving and had not told them. The elder later revealed that they beat her because of this.

In the year 1930, at the age of twenty-seven, he left the world with all its vanity behind and went to the Holy Mountain to become a monk. His abundant zeal and search for a higher ascetic life led him to Karoulia, a dreadful place, the driest and most unforgiving location on Athos. At the time Father Seraphim lived there, in a cave with a small church dedicated to the archangels. When Father Seraphim was a young monk he had disobeyed his elder Gabriel, the founder of the hermitage, and God had allowed him to become possessed. His elder had addressed the icon of the archangel with pain in his heart:

"What is this, my holy archangel?"

At that moment he heard a voice from the icon saying, "I am disciplining this disobedient monk, so that he may be corrected and reformed."

Humbly, Elder Gabriel replied, "Ah, but now let us heal him." And immediately, Father Seraphim was relieved from the tyranny of the devil and became healthy.

There was a time when Father Seraphim argued with his elder, and the elder threw him out. Father Seraphim sought advice from a certain spiritual father who told him, "Go back, my child. Prostrate yourself with as much humility as possible, because the devil has set about to damn one of you, if he cannot damn both, and know that the end is drawing near for one of you." Father Seraphim did as he was told, and a short time after their reconciliation Elder Gabriel fell asleep in the Lord.

And so, the young George became subordinate to Elder Seraphim and struggled in obedience and self-denial, seeking ever increasing asceticism.

He was tonsured on March 17, 1933 and was given the name Gabriel, both in honor of the archangel to whom the hermitage was dedicated, and in memory of his grandfather Gabriel.

He lived with his elder as a disciple for six years. On the day of his tonsure Father Gabriel saw a demon in the form of an ape jumping up on him. "Elder," he yelled, "an ape!" "Tell him to return to the unceasing fire," Elder Seraphim told him, and as Father Gabriel was repeating it, the monkey demon immediately disappeared.

Elder Seraphim fell asleep in the Lord after the service of vespers one afternoon. As Father Gabriel read "Through the prayers...", the elder peacefully passed away. With respect and love the young monk buried him and having his elder's blessing as a provision, as he had served him and comforted him, he thereafter devoted himself to ever greater struggles.

He would sleep on boards, with a rock for a pillow. He undertook great fasts, being a faster to the extreme. His typical diet consisted of rusks; he did not even eat legumes, as he considered them a luxury and a pleasure. He only ate rusks, a few ground almonds, and figs in

August. He planted a vine and gave the grapes to others, pretending that he could not eat them because he had no teeth. He also ate wild greens and radishes. He did not consume non-fasting food even on Pascha, quoting the apostolic saying, "Every man that striveth for the mastery is temperate in all things" perceiving it in a temporal sense.[1] One year he happened to be at the monastery of Dionysiou for Pascha, and after the service he asked for the leftovers from Holy Week. When they told him that they had thrown them out, he ate bread and olives for the day of the Resurrection.

There was a time when he attended a meal at a monastery on a non-fasting day. He did not break his fasting rule, eating only bread and olives. Another time at a communal monastery meal they served dessert. When they offered him some, he said, "Take these snots away."

He rarely ate anything non-fasting, even on non-fasting days. For the last fourteen years of his life he fasted from oil as well. At the end of his life, when they asked him why he fasted so much, he answered: "Well, sometimes I ate non-fasting food, but I did not benefit from it at all. When I was a layman, I ate a lot, so now I fast."

Indeed, he fasted so much that some called him a faster and others condemned him as deluded. Father Gabriel from the monastery of Dionysiou would say, "He was a great faster, very violent."[2] Father Gerontius from the community of the Danielites said, "He was one of the great ascetics, very violent, but sometimes extreme." Other contemporary sources included Father Païsius ("He was a real ascetic"), Elder Hilarion ("it is worthwhile to write about Elder Gabriel"), and Father Gregory of the Danielites: "He took asceticism to the extreme. A great ascetic. He worked hard, there, in the stone steps outside his hut. He communed at every Divine Liturgy since he such was a great faster."

At some point the Danielites had a memorial service for their elder and sent a young man to Elder Gabriel with some food. When the elder saw it, he said, "My dear child, why did you make such an

1   The word "πάντα", here rendered as "[in] all things", which is its meaning in Ancient Greek, also means "always" in Modern Greek. —ED.
2   See Mt. 11:12: "the kingdom Heaven suffereth violence, and the violent take it by force." —ED.

effort? Glory to God, this year He gave me so many blessings. I have soooo many potatoes," and he showed the young man two or three kilos of potatoes the size of eggs. To the ascetic elder boiled potatoes seemed a feast. When he ate fava beans he ate them with the peels. He also planted mallow, which he ate raw. Another time, when the Danielites sent him something, he sent them back mallow, advising them not to eat it raw, but to boil it.

One year, on the feastday of his patron saint, he went to the Danielites and asked them for a handful of rice so that he could eat a little rice without oil to show reverence for the day.

He had an earthenware jar with flour in his cell, which he had covered with a cloth tied around the mouth with some rope. One time, when a visitor was there, he said, "Let's see if the thieves (the ants) stole my flour." He opened the jar and verified that they had not stolen it. He did this so that the visitor would see that the elder had flour, so he would think that he kneaded and ate warm bread.

Every night he did a vigil for six to eight hours. He made a path outside his cell about half a meter wide and forty to fifty meters long, which he covered with gravel. At night he walked on that path saying the Jesus prayer so that sleep would not overtake him. He put boulders and tree stumps along the side, so that he could sit when he got tired. He worked hard to make that path, as he was afraid to use the existing paths near his cell. because which were hewn along the precipice and he was afraid the devil would throw him over the edge. When he did a vigil in his cell he held himself up by a rope which he had fastened to two places in the ceiling. He also did countless prostrations, going up and down like a spring.

When he finished his six-hour vigil he would cense the icons and his little chapel while chanting: "When the thrones are placed and the books are opened and God sitteth in judgment...", remembering the day of judgment. In order to have remembrance of death he had prepared his tomb near the shrine of the Virgin Mary between Saint Anne and Little Saint Anne. Someone went and wrote "a work of satanic delusion" next to this tomb. Seeing it, he consulted with his spiritual father, Gabriel the abbot of Dionysiou, and following his advice he filled the tomb in.

He assiduously avoided idle talk. An acquaintance of his, a priest, desired to visit him. When he was told, he replied: "If you want to talk about spiritual things, come. We can discuss such things all day and all night. But I don't have time for idle talk." He was a man of silence. He would speak and give advice only if they asked him. He had the grace of teaching.

He had learned the dangers of the passion of judgment from experience, and he avoided it. There was a time that he criticized another monk and the devil tormented him with extreme sleepiness that whole night. He was shaken by that temptation and thoroughly understood the words of Saint John's *Ladder of Divine Ascent*, "If we have formed the habit of judging, we can be utterly ruined by this alone."[3]

Visitors could not find him easily, as he would hide in the rocks. He avoided them, as they bombarded him with pointless questions: "Where are you from? What do you eat? How do you pass your time?" et cetera. The elder would say, "Is this the reason I came here? To waste my time? I came here to have continuous communion with the Lord and pray constantly."

Sometimes the following would also happen, as he himself would later narrate: "Different people would come to my cell for conversation. I would be sitting on the rocks, they would pass by right next to me, nearly bump into me, but they could not see me." The elder had prayed and God had made him invisible to those interested in nonsense.

The most reverend Metropolitan of Veroia and Naousa Panteleiemon described his first visit to Elder Gabriel, when he was still a young student in the Athoniada.[4] The then young man had corresponded with the elder previously, and, as he later recounted, "following the instructions of the Danielites, after quite a long hike, I arrived at the cell of Father Gabriel on the steep slopes of Athos. I knocked on the door and waited. No answer. I knocked again, but still only silence. I shouted, 'Father Gabriel, I am John Kalpakidis.' Nothing. Complete silence. All I could see around me were the sharp

---

3   *The Ladder of Divine Ascent*, 10:15
4   A boys' school on Athos (at Karyes). —TRANS.

rocks and the sea. Following the advice of Father Nephon I sat and
I began to chant "O Theotokos and Virgin," the supplicatory canon
to the Panagia, and whatever else I could remember. The time was
passing, but the door of the cell remained closed, and it did not seem
that Father Gabriel was coming. It got to noon, and the door suddenly
opened and he stood there. He asked:

"'You are still here?'

"Excitedly, I replied:

"'Why would I leave, father, and where would I go? I came for
you. I wanted to meet you.'

"'Come inside' he said to me.

"I looked around. How was I supposed to go in? There was no
room at all in the elder's cell. There was only a plank, and behind
that a vast chasm. Understanding my predicament, the elder quickly
explained that a little while ago a boulder had rolled down the mountain and demolished the greater part of his cell and chapel, so now
he slept inside a barrel. He prayed to Christ and the Panagia to have
an angel hold another rock that was ready to fall, because if it, too,
fell it would destroy the rest of the cell.

"I went in and situated myself as best as I could. I sat, and the
elder began speaking to me about the Panagia, about her visit to
Athos, about her protection and care for the monks, and afterwards he
turned the discussion to the topic of noetic prayer and the asceticism
of the fathers. I sat transfixed and listened to him piously, without
interrupting him for a long time.

"At some point I looked down to check my watch. The elder saw
it and asked me:

"'Are you in a hurry to leave?'

"'No, geronda' I told him, 'but the Danielites told me to get back
in time for the meal.'

"Surprised at my answer, he turned to me and said:

"'Well, I am giving you the heart of the book and you want to eat
the cover? Don't worry, I'll cook for you today.'

"Saddened by my mistake, I immediately asked forgiveness and
added:

"'No, Elder, I'll stay here. I came to meet you and I want to listen to whatever you tell me.'

"The elder continued speaking to me about the mysteries of noetic prayer and I listened to him silently, without a word. When mealtime came, he got up and brought a clean empty tin and a bottle which contained some liquid. 'I'll give you something to drink,' he said pouring some liquid from the bottle into the can, 'and if you like it, I'll give you some more.'

"Without knowing what it was, I drank it, but unaccustomed as I was, it settled like a stone in my stomach.

"'Would you like some more?' Father Gabriel asked me. I replied:

"'No thank you, Elder.'

"'You don't like it', he concluded.

"'I like it, but I don't want more, thank you,' I added.

"The liquid he had offered me was prickly pear juice, and that was his food, as he never ate oil. I later heard that at some point a young man went to become a monk near him, and after a long while had passed and he had asked him about different things, he wondered, 'When do we eat oil, *geronda*?', to which the elder replied, 'Not even on Pascha.' The life he led was so harsh, so strict, that he subjected himself to indescribable trials.

"My meeting with Elder Gabriel created the first flicker of desire in my soul to become a permanent resident of the Holy Mountain. The elder was the holiest thing I had met up to that point in my life."

Unceasing prayer was the primary task of Elder Gabriel. In order to fight against the devil with unceasing prayer he went to a cave which was high up, on the right side of the cobblestone road, as one goes up from the jetty. Some days he would go and hide there in order to give himself over to his beloved noetic prayer undisturbed. It was a hollow of a rock built up in front with dry stones. He had a wide board for a bed and a tree stump wrapped in pieces of cloth for a pillow. There was no path to get there.

He went to liturgy at Saint Anne's and wherever else he could. One time, as he was returning from liturgy in the morning, he met an old priest, an acquaintance of his, on the road. His eyes seemed tired from the vigil, but he was extremely joyful, and could not hide the joy he was experiencing. He said emphatically, "Father, these atomic weapons that the people in the world have today are nothing: we have greater weapons! Prayer and Holy Communion give us inner fire, 'like fire-breathing lions.' How can the devil draw near? We partake and he turns to dust, he flees far away, whoosh!" Every so often he would also celebrate the Divine Liturgy in his cell.

There was a time when he invited Father Ephraim for a liturgy. Fr Ephraim, thinking that he may also want to do a memorial service for his elder, went an hour early. Elder Gabriel said to him angrily, "Father, what time did I tell you to come? Do you know of what honey from heaven I was partaking and you came and interrupted me?" Another time he told Father Ephraim: "You can not imagine what love I feel when I am praying for those at sea. When I see a small boat it's as though God is telling me, 'You do well to pray'."

He tried to commune often, every day if possible. He was always prepared for Holy Communion, since he always fasted, did vigils, and prayed, cultivating repentance and humility. The fathers had said to him that if one wanted to commune often he should not eat oil, and he applied it absolutely.

He had the practice of silence, and after Divine Liturgies in his cell he would not say a word, not even to the priest. He would make a prostration to him, give him a tin of calamari (his compensation) and go to his cell.

He had great experience with demonic temptations. One time Father M. said to him, "I want to see the temptation so I can believe it exists." "If you see what is truly there," the elder answered, "you will die from fear." There was a time when Elder Gabriel was praying, and he saw demons as swarms of wasps attacking him.

As though his daily and nightly ascetic struggles and great fasts were not enough, Elder Gabriel strove for even higher levels of asceticism, thoroughly wearing himself out through the day. He split rocks, built garden beds, sifted dirt, and moved it great distances. One planter he made had a thousand buckets of sifted dirt, another one thousand five hundred, another two thousand five hundred. Such labor from an ascetic who was hardly more than skin and bones! When he became sweaty from his manual labor and prostrations, he would simply change his undershirt and continue. Being moved by love, he would sometimes go and sift dirt at night, secretly (so that others would not notice him), and he would bring it to the other ascetics in the area. In that rocky and inhospitable area dirt was valuable, as the monks could plant some fava beans or some wild cabbage. Elder Gabriel underwent all his labor and effort as a gift, in order to give some rest to the fathers. He planted almond trees and a fig tree in planters near the stream. Potatoes and fava beans as well. Someone asked him, "Elder, why are you putting those trees here?" He answered, "I'll leave at some point, but some passerby will come, eat of them, and say, 'May God forgive the sins of the man who planted these'."

Among these things he also planted a rosebush. When they asked him why this rosebush was needed in the desert, he answered, "You know, when I go to Saint Anne's and pass by the shrine of the Panagia, I bow and leave our mother a rose." This harsh and rough ascetic had so much sensitivity that it brought him joy to give a hard-earned rose to the Panagia.

It was this love and sensitivity which made him care even for the birds of heaven. He took his chisel and made a little cistern on the boulder near his cell and flattened the surface next to it, forming a little table. Twice a day he put rainwater in the little cistern and dry bread on the flat surface, setting a table for the little birds.

He clapped his hands and called out in a special way and flocks of blackbirds, doves, and other birds flew to him. They would eat, drink, and bathe in the little cistern, and once they were satisfied they would fly away and other birds would come. He had a robin, who he called 'Lalouli,' with whom he was more familiar and of whom he took special care.

During the Greek Civil War Elder Gabriel was helping a certain constable named Christos who was hiding in the caves of Little Saint Anne's near the port in the area of Katounakia. He brought him food, rain or shine, but the man was demon-possessed, and one day he took a hammer and smashed it down next to the elder's head in anger saying, "You shouldn't have brought me bread." "From that point on he had the legion inside him," Elder Gabriel would say.

He foreknew and foretold many things. His brother was a novice with him for a period of time, but then chose to leave and return to the world. Elder Gabriel told him that he would curse the day he left for the world. Indeed, the prophecy was fulfilled. His brother was ambushed by a faction of communists and they impaled him.

There was another man that showed him a handful of liras[5] saying, "This is what has value." The elder considered him a materialist and a Mason and foretold that his end was near. Within a few days he died.

He once saw a certain layman, a worker in Kafsokalyvia, and called out to him by the name of his village, though he had never met him before.

One day a young man came to his hermitage and begged the elder to keep him as a disciple. Even though he wanted a disciple, the elder sent him away, as he perceived a spiritually foul odor emanating from him. The later life of that young man justified Elder Gabriel's decision and proved the power of his spiritual gift. The man became a monk, but later renounced the schema[6], got married, and became an enemy of monks, an enemy of holy things, and an enemy of God.

For a period in the beginning of his monastic life Elder Gabriel was a zealot. He had joined a faction of zealots and was not in communion with the monasteries or the Church. During that period he had a hardness and fanaticism about him, and because of the combination of his character, age, and zealotry he was sharp and brittle, occasionally even clashing with his elder and the other fathers. Later he calmed down and softened. His friend, Elder Symeon of Kafsokalyvia, helped him to leave the faction of zealots. He read Saint Isaac the Syrian's fifty-first homily to him, "On the harm of foolish zeal".

---

5   A kind of currency. —TRANS.
6   I.e. his monastic vows and commitment. —TRANS.

The chapel of the Archangels

The cell of Elder Gabriel

At one point, as he was participating in the Divine Liturgy at the Lavra, during the hymn "We praise Thee" he felt an exceeding amount of compunction and perceived that he must follow the Church and not, as he had thought until then, the zealots.

He definitively and irrevocably abandoned the zealots in 1955. He later explained to Father Bessarion the lodge-master of Dionysiou: "I'll tell you my story. I told myself, starting today, I am changing. I will no longer be a zealot. I saw that my mind [nous] was not clear, my prayer was clouded. So I considered, 'What is wrong with me? What is harming me?' So one day I thought I would go and attend liturgy with those celebrating it. I went to Stavronikita and attended liturgy. The celebrant was Father Evthymius the elder (from the community of the Crucified). He celebrates there every Sunday. Just after the liturgy, something happened to me: my mind [nous] cleared, and I decided from that day on that I would not return to the zealots. I had been deluded and did not know it. Now, however, I've understood."

So Father Gabriel left behind the foolish zeal which is "not according to knowledge" but kept the zeal for matters of faith and tradition.

There was once a discussion in which Elder Gabriel was indignant listening to some Protestant theories. Suddenly lighting struck a rock about eight meters away and interrupted the fruitless discussion.

During a certain feast, someone told him that the "Dynamis" that the chanters chanted was an innovation, so he chided the chanters.

One time he met a priest smoking on the road. He berated and censured him saying, "Are you a priest or a *karagiozis*?[7]"

He often prayed to God asking, "Lord, send me a sinner so I that can graft him into Thy grace."

There was a young man studying theology who loved monasticism and asked Elder Gabriel whether he should finish his degree or become a monk. The elder answered, "First finish your degree, and then you can follow your calling" (to become a monk). The

---

7   A comical character in Greek and Turkish puppetry; in this case, one who treats his priestly vocation as a joke. —TRANS.

visiting youth made a prostration and lived with the elder for about one hundred days before returning. The elder made concessions for him, relaxing his own stringent ascetic practices by eating legumes, though without any oil. He counseled him often: "I want you to have cherubic eyes, not sleepy eyes. I want your mind to be sharp. When you become a monk I will give you the best name, but you better take care that you honor it!"

He advocated obedience, which he himself had perfected during his six-year discipleship to his elder Seraphim and from studying ascetic literature. He read the Philokalia and particularly loved the *Evergetinos*,[8] about which he said, "I have read the *Evergetinos* eighteen times, and if I live I'll read it eighteen more. You do not need any other book. You get an answer for every question from this one. The consensus of the fathers is found in its pages." He would ask his spiritual father, Abbot Gabriel of Dionysiou, about everything, and for simple matters he would be advised by Elder Christodoulos of Katounakia, the shoemaker. He would later tell his own disciple, "Your elder is your God. If you've seen your elder, you've seen your God. If your elder tells you to go jump into the sea you may ask once, 'are you sure, elder? I should go jump into the sea?' and if he tells you to go jump a second time, then you should jump.

He also said, "If you take care of an elder in his old age, the holy God will send a man to look after you in your old age as well."

He would not allow his disciple to handle musical books, converse with others, or chant at liturgy. When there was a need, the elder chanted himself.

His disciple was memorizing troparia, but the elder forbade him from doing it.

There was a time when he and his disciple visited an acquaintance of his at Saint Anne's, Elder Arsenius, who knit thick woolen socks for a living. They sat silently for a while and then left without saying a word. How did the two elders communicate?

The novice could not endure the harsh life of Elder Gabriel of Karoulia and wanted to leave. The elder sent him to his friend, the

---

8   A large, popular collection of sayings and teachings of the ascetic Desert Fathers. —TRANS.

abbot Gabriel of Dionysiou, where he stayed and became a monk. He would later say, "He deserved the break. He was extremely obedient."

For his help in matters of a spiritual nature, the monks of Dionysiou would give him some necessary things. Out of love, the fathers would say, "Have some more dessert, Father Gabriel, and take some oil!" but keeping to his monastic practice he took only the absolute necessities, saying, "If I take more, I must do more praying for you on my prayer-rope." He only wanted what was necessary, and he repaid it either in kind or through prayer.

He supported the young monks of Dionysiou in their spiritual journey and would call them "my grafts." He advised Father Symeon to read Abba Dorotheos and pray the Jesus prayer "like a machine gun." He would respectfully tell the then holy abbot, "Elder, do not go out into the world, because it is then that the devil dives into your flock." He gave a "*patsavoura*," that is, a temporary rule of silence, to another young monk.

A monk at Dionysiou once asked him, "I am contemplating leaving for the desert," to which the elder answered, "no, you're not cut out for the desert. Stay and work out your salvation here at the monastery."

Elder Bessarion of Dionysiou used to say: "Elder Gabriel was a virtuous man, a holy man. His cassocks weren't anything special. They were old, worn, but without patches. He did not speak with anyone. He fasted constantly. He did not consume oil. He would often come to the refectory, but only took a little bread for his cell. He counseled me regarding what a monk should be. He told me to be careful, to say the Jesus prayer. Sometimes he would tell me some of the things he saw. He once told me that he saw a monk who had two apes with him, one on the one side and one on the other. He did not tell me his name, but I understood who it was, as that monk had created many scandals.

"At times he would come to Dionysiou and confess to the abbot. They gave him a cell in the guest house, but he did not sleep there. As soon as the sacristan opened the church to light the lamps, Elder Gabriel would go in. Sometimes they had spiritual discussions. The sacristan once asked him, 'Elder Gabriel, I see that you like our monastery; why don't you stay here?'

"'Now you force me to tell you things that you cannot understand,' said the elder. 'I see people's souls, and I see some that have devils on them, and seeing these things I fall into judgment, and on account of this I cannot remain here long.'"

Elder Gabriel had acquired experience and spiritual knowledge from his struggles, his study of ascetic literature, and the Jesus prayer. He had the grace of God and divine consolation. The joy he had from divine grace was a normal state for him. He was always joyful.

Elder Gabriel would say: "God gave me a spiritual gift and I lost it. I hope by the end He will give it back to me." His gifts included speaking like a rhetorician and manual construction.

Here are some of the teachings and counsels of Elder Gabriel:

"I learned the monastic life from falling down and getting back up."

"The signs of stillness are self-control, silence, and self-accusation" (Saint Gregory of Sinai).

"Now that you are young you should struggle to fast, do your prayer rule, and do your prostrations, because when you get old you will not be able to do anything."

"Violence, violence, salvation."[9]

He would express the power of the divine law in simple words (for example, "God is the Lord of vengeance"), and he emphasized repentance as medicine for the healing of those who had fallen away. He would say, "The Lord says, 'Either get yourself straightened out, or I'll do it Myself'."

Being humble, he would say, "I hope to become a lightless star in the noetic firmament."

"When we suffer, let us not say that we are suffering for the love of Christ, but for our own sins.".

"God sees the depths of the soul; the other things do not interest Him."

---

9   These words form a rhyme in Greek: "Βία, βία, σωτηρία." Cf. Mt. 11:12.—ED.

When someone told him that it is possible that the communist faction may prevail in the Greek Civil War, and if so, they would slaughter them all, he answered: "Blessed be the hour," revealing his desire for martyrdom and proclaiming God's glory. He loved Saint Maximos the Confessor very much and whenever he mentioned his name he was completely filled with delight.

He would describe the censure of our conscience with a word from his homeland, "*xourafakoula*," which means "little razors," which prick and sting inside us when we sin.

Elder Gabriel was strong-willed and had great stamina. During liturgy and vigil he would stand upright like a column. As the years passed, however, health problems began to appear. He suffered great pain in his lower back.

There was a period when he was bedridden for seven days. As soon as Elder Gerontius of the Danielites learned about it, he took him some medicine and made him some soup, thinking that being on his own for so many days he would not have eaten anything. When he offered them to Elder Gabriel, the old monk refused to take anything and answered him: "Elder, which is stronger, your pills and soup or the grace of God? If God wishes He will heal me; if not, He will take me." The next day they saw him healthy, working on his garden beds.

Later, once he had become permanently confined to his bed due to the back pain, he suffered horrific pain alone in the desert. He would be heard saying the Jesus prayer out loud, "Lord Jesus Christ have mercy on me," interrupted by sighs of pain, "aaah...."

When someone asked how he was doing, he answered, "A cross without nails." That is, he suffered greatly as if he were being crucified without nails.

He had once taken a piece of paper and on it he had written advice regarding the way he should face his death. Now he saw it truly nearing, even though he had spent his whole life contemplating and preparing for it.

When he could no longer take care of himself, the Danielites wanted to take him in in order to care for him in his old age, but he did not want to leave his cell. At that point he asked Father Hilarion to occasionally come and help him. The monk obliged, and asked him frequently if he wanted any soup, rice, or porridge, but all the elder wanted was boiled potatoes, which he ate with sea salt gathered from the salt pans. He had to feed him, as the elder's hands could no longer move.

Elder Hilarion narrated: "One day he told me to fill a little rock cistern with water, and at sunset, just as I put in the water, different birds, robins, chaffinches, blackbirds, and a great many others gathered, filling the area. They drank water, bathed and flew around Elder Gabriel. They would sit and look him in the eyes. He saw my perplexity and said to me, 'These are my pets. I've taught them to come at sunset.' When I later told him, 'Elder Gabriel, you are old and sick now. Eat a little oil. See these boiled potatoes? Wouldn't they be better with a little oil?'

"'You think I don't know they would be better? And if we had fish, I know it would be even better than that. But I got over these things back when I was a constable. I'd eat half a roast lamb in one sitting, so since I will have to give an account for that, I try and make up for whatever I can now.'

"'But doesn't it bother you when they talk about you not eating oil?'

"'I do not care about such things, they do not interest me, let them say whatever they want. I do not look at what others say but at the sorry state of my own soul and how it will cross the river of fire. There was a time when a spiritual father told me to eat oil, both so the other fathers would stop talking about me, and because I'd start feeling differently, physically. Well, I decided to try it, so one time at a feast at Saint Anne's I sat at the refectory. They had fish that day, and they placed a full portion for me. I was hungry and ate the whole thing. Then the other fathers were saying, "Elder Gabriel sat down at the refectory. What happened? And he's eating; how is that possible?" So before they were talking about how and why I do not eat oil, and now they were talking about how and why I do. I did not feel different, neither better nor worse, so I told all this to my spiritual father and did not eat oil again after that.'"

When Elder Gabriel became completely incapacitated, he agreed to go to the Danielites, and they carried him up in a stretcher. Until that point he had the custom of communing every day. He had a blessing from his spiritual father to do so, and he had a portion of consecrated Host in his little chapel. The Danielites, however, disagreed:

"Look, father, we cannot accept this, to commune you every day".

"Look," he told them: "as long as I lived in my cell I did what I wanted, but it is one thing to live alone there and another to live in community here. I will follow your own practices and do as you say.

Marveling at his answer, the fathers replied:

"Father, you can have communion however frequently you wish."

The brotherhood of the Danielites, known for their princely love for all, cared for him in his last days and communed him every day.

The steel body of the ascetic of Karoulia, the body that crushed boulders and performed great fasts, was finally defeated by exhaustion, age, and illness, and lay supine and weak. His fighting spirit, however, was still strong as ever, undefeated. He even ordered the monks: "Fathers, if I lose my mind and ask to eat oil, do not give it to me, and bring me neither doctor nor medicine. My whole hope is in God."

While on his sickbed praying and thinking on his sins, he was moved to a state of ecstasy. He saw a vision of Paradise and cried out loud, "Wow! What is this I am seeing! Such flowers, such beauty! Are these beautiful things made for man? Wow! Do you see? Do you?" Fr Daniel would reply, "We don't see anything, Elder." Then, trying to hide the grace of the vision, he would say, "Oh, I don't see anything either." The day before he had seen another vision. He told Father Hilarion, "I am seeing signs and wonders." It seems that the good God, in his righteous judgment, rewarded his great self-denial and informed him of his salvation while he was still living.

He was praying constantly, and in his mind he was already living in the next world. Once, when he seemed to be asleep and they were speaking to him and woke him up, he reproached them saying, "Ah, why did you interrupt me?".

When the monks told him that his feastday was approaching, he answered that he would not be with them. He foresaw his death. One day he asked to commune, and when they told him that it was still Matins, and so the Host had not been consecrated, he told them to commune him with the presanctified Gifts, as he knew that by the time of Liturgy he would have departed for the next life.

The fathers communed him and gathered around him. Since the time for the service was approaching, he told them: "Go on, leave me here and go to the service. Go." However, while at church the abbot thought, "This man is in his final moments and we are leaving him on his own?" And quickly returning, he saw Elder Gabriel breathing his last.

He fell asleep on November 3, 1968.

He had a holy end. All the possessionless ascetic left behind in his hut were a few kilos of almonds. That was his only inheritance, and he told Father Hilarion to give them to a priest as recompense for performing a few memorial services for his soul. But everyone held memorial services for the holy elder, without having to be asked.

After three years, when they did the transfer of the relics, his remains had become like ash; perhaps because he did not eat any oil.

May we have his blessing. Amen.

Kostas, the fool for Christ

Kostas Kaviotis, the Fool for Christ

Everyone in the community of Karyes knew Kostas and showed him love and compassion. They would see him walking around Karyes, regularly going to liturgy at the Protaton,[1] doing his crazy things, and they were all puzzled. Is he crazy? Does he suffer from an actual mental disorder, or is he a fool for Christ?[2] His peaceful and bright—though unwashed—face, and some wise and prescient things he said, made it difficult for the fathers to know. He was quiet, pure, mild. He did not bother anybody or ask anything of anyone.

But who was Kostas? Was he a monk or a layman? This was an inscrutable mystery.

He was born on February 10, 1898, in the village of Kalensi, in the area of Dodoni in Epirus. His parents were named Stavros and Anthoula Angeli. He went to the monastery of Dionysiou to become a monk, and remained there for a while as a novice. Later, he came to Karyes and lived as a *kaviotis*[3] in a derelict cell at Sarai[4]. He wore a monastic cap, had a beard and long hair, and so looked like a monk. Instead of a cassock, however, he wore an overcoat. In the winter he went about nearly naked, dressed only in tattered rags that went down to his knees, and in the summer he wore a greatcoat fastened at the

---

1   The church of the president of the monastic republic on Athos and major church for Karyes. —TRANS.

2   A saint with a high calling by God to be seemingly insane, who yet provides great spiritual instruction.—TRANS.

3   A monk who is registered with a certain monastic community, to which he belongs, but lives outside the monastery proper in a cell which belongs to the monastery, either for free or by paying a minuscule amount of rent.—TRANS.

4   The Skete of St. Andrew.—TRANS.

waist with rope. He never bathed, and he never washed his clothes. When the filth on the clothes was too much to bear, he hung them outside to be cleaned in the rain, and once they dried, he wore them again.

He used to visit Father Gabriel Makkavos, who felt sorry for him and gave him food. Father Gabriel would also put flea powder on his clothes, as the fleas were eating Kostas alive.

Kostas had a "*bakratsi*"[5] (a tin can with wire for a handle), and for this reason some called him "bakratsos" (the *bakratsi*-bearer). He would go to konakia or to cells and wait outside for hours, without knocking or disturbing the tenant, until the latter would open the door on his own for whatever reason he needed. These monks understood and would put some food in his bakratsi. Whatever they gave him, soup, dessert, salad, he mixed together, and sometimes filling the rest of his bakratsi with water, he would make a prostration, thank them, and leave.

He would go to the monastery of Koutloumousi and sit with the fathers in the dining room, always entering last. He would take four or five portions of food and mix them all up. At times he would break out in sobs and tears, and at other times burst into laughter. The abbot, Father Macarius, greatly respected him, and told the young monk who was in charge of the dining hall: "Treat Kostas as you would your own eyes. Take care of him, and give him whatever he asks."

There was a cemetery across from the Protaton, and at times the fathers would see him standing for one or two hours, facing the cemetery, not moving at all. They would hear him murmur and grimace, but they could not understand what he was saying. Was he perhaps praying for the reposed?

There were times when he did the same thing in the middle of the road. He just sat and murmured. His mind was somewhere else, engrossed in the things he was murmuring. The more spiritual of the fathers believed that he was reciting verses from the Psalter, or that his mind was taken up to heaven and he did not understand that

5   A small copper pot.—TRANS.

people were near him. When people spoke to him, he would come to himself, make some gesture, do something foolish, and leave, hiding his spiritual work.

Bishop Chrysostom of Rodostolos, who lived at Sarai for years, had a well-intentioned curiosity about Kostas and his life, and trying to learn more about him he would occasionally watch him. He heard him reciting the service of Vespers from memory, without a book or even any light, even chanting the correct "Lord, I have cried," resurrectional troparia, and hymns to the Theotokos for that particular Sunday.[6]

There was a time when Kostas had left his cell, and some monks went in to explore. Imagine their surprise when they found Kostas inside. As they stood there, embarrassed, he simply told them to venerate four large, life-size, full-body icons he had. They asked for his forgiveness, and he told them, "Go in peace. May Christ be with you." While they were in his cell they did not see a table, bed, blankets, pillows, or even basic heating. And all that, considering that winter in Karyes is particularly harsh, even with heating.

All these things made the bishop of Rodostolos respect and revere Elder Kostas greatly.

Very few understood his spiritual state, but even they did not comprehend the depth of his spirituality.

Most of the fathers assisted him in various ways out of sympathy, but unfortunately there were a few that held him in contempt or even mocked him. One or two even tormented him in order to get a laugh at his expense. There was a time when one of these saw Kostas coming along the path which passed below the balcony of his cell. He filled a bucket with water, and when Kostas was directly below the balcony, he emptied the bucket on him, soaking him from head to toe. Elder Kostas continued on his way undisturbed, as though nothing had happened, not even looking up to see who had done that to him. Who would endure such a thing without complaint?

All ascetic struggles are difficult and require effort, but few more so than obedience. According to the holy fathers it is a denial of one's

6   Bishop Chrysostom of Rodostolos, *Πρόσωπα καὶ δρώμενα στὸν Ἄθωνα*, Mt. Athos 2000, ibid. p. 186-195.

own soul, the equal to being a confessor. Yet one of the things that exceed even obedience is the life of holy foolishness, as the fool for Christ becomes "the offscouring of all things,"[7] is "humbled exceedingly,"[8] and tramples his pride into oblivion. Foolishness for Christ requires a specific calling from God, and these "fools" are loved by God, because they take up this heavy cross[9] for His love. And because of their great humility, God reveals His mysteries to them.

The fathers believed that Elder Kostas was this very type of fool for Christ and that he hid a spiritual secret.

An elderly monk from Karyes explained: "One day, when I was a young monk, around 20 or 22 years old, I was at Father Stephen's workshop. I was joking and laughing with him when Elder Kostas came in. When Father Stephen stepped out for a moment, Elder Kostas looked at me seriously and said: "Monks do not laugh." I immediately stopped, but as soon as Father Stephen returned, he began acting like a fool again. His solemnity and his counsel made an impression on me. A crazy man does not speak in such a way."

Later, Kostas left Sarai and lived in an abandoned cell called "Philadelphos" near the community of Saint George, outside Karyes. The cell did not have doors, windows, or even a floor. There was only an old half-destroyed door as an entrance. He walked on the wooden beams on the floor, and slept at the edge of the cell's small church, in the area of the minuscule altar. It is truly inexplicable how he endured during the winter. Humanly, it would have been impossible, but it seems he was covered by the grace of God.

He had an old Triodion,[10] from which he chanted, and a leather-bound Bible. At some point, when the elder was not in his cell, someone passing by saw it and, desiring it, stole it. Kostas met this same person on the road, and said to him: "You took my Bible. You should go bring it back to me quickly." The thief was completely taken aback and shocked, and wondered how he knew, as he was

---

7   1 Corinthians 4:13. —TRANS.

8   Psalm 115:1.—TRANS.

9   Matthew 16:24—TRANS.

10   Service book containing the hymns and rubrics for the Lenten season, pre-Lenten season, and Holy Week.—TRANS.

not there and had not seen him. He came to believe that Kostas had grace from God, and while living in a spiritual state, pretended to be a fool.

There was a time when Elder Kostas went to a young student of the Athoniada and quietly revealed a sin that the student had committed, telling him he should not fall into that sin again.

Another time, a young monk asked him:

"Tell me, Constantine, are you a monk?"

The elder answered monosyllabically:

"Yes."

"And where did you become a monk?"

"At Dionysiou."

"And what was your monastic name?"

"Akakios"

"Where are you from?"

"The islands."

"From which island?"

"Rhodes."

When, however, the monk continued to ask him about details and other things that happened in his life, he began to speak nonsense.

Had he in fact been tonsured a monk, or did he simply feel that he was a monk? Were the things he said spoken evasively, or did he mean them in a different way?

When Elder Damascene from the monastic community of Saint Basil first ran into him at Kapsala, Kostas called him out by name without knowing him. They spoke, and Elder Kostas confidentially told him that he hailed from Asia Minor, but that his exact genealogy was never known. He confided that he was a theologian and a mediocre author. When Elder Damascene asked him about something that had been occupying his mind, Elder Kostas replied, "You are still stuck on that, old man? Whoever does not struggle with this particular *logismos*[11] does not become a monk." His simple words reassured Elder Damascene.

---

11 A provocative thought from the evil one which gives birth to temptation.—TRANS.

In the end, Elder Kostas was not crazy as some thought, but a theologian and an author of two books: *Man: The Flower of Heaven* and *Earth, and Athos: How I Knew It and How I Leave It.*[12]

The day that they voted for the new article of the charter of Mount Athos[13], Kostas, then a youth and only in the beginning stages of his foolishness for Christ, went up to the bell tower of the Protaton and started ringing the bells in a mournful manner. He later explained the incident and his reasoning behind it to Elder Damascene of Saint Basil's:

"Elder Damascene, you know that this place is dedicated to our Panagia. Our common mother enlightened the builders of all the holy venerable places, and they, in turn, asked the patriarchs and the emperors to allow Mount Athos to remain free, without rulers or lords, not bound or supervised by ecclesiastical or political authorities. This preferential form of government was guaranteed by the Holy Typicon of the Goat[14], other patriarchal sigillia[15], imperial chrysobulls[16], and firmans[17] from the sultans. Aside from these perpetual guarantor documents, Mount Athos is ruled by Holy Tradition, which is based on the Scriptures, and on the precepts and counsels of the Holy Fathers who died in sanctity. Most importantly, it functions in an Orthodox manner. It is the Orthodox heart of the Athonite conscience. This common conscience checks itself and understands the consequences of its actions. So, neither penal codes nor penal magistrates were

---

12   See Archim. Evdokimus Karakoulakis, Διοίκηση καὶ ὀργάνωση τοῦ Ἁγίου Ὄρους, Holy Mountain 2007, p. 198-199.

13   May 10, 1924—TRANS.

14   The very first typicon of Mount Athos, signed by the Roman Emperor John Tzimiskes and Saint Athanasius the Athonite in AD 972. It is called the Typikon of the Tragos (goat), as it was written on a goat-skin parchment.—TRANS.

15   A type of legal document publicly affirmed with a seal, usually of lead. It originated in the Roman Empire in the ninth century.—TRANS.

16   A golden bull or chrysobull was a decree issued by Roman Emperors. The term was originally coined for the golden seal attached to the decree but came to be applied to the entire decree. Such decrees were known as golden bulls in western Europe and chrysobullos logos, or chrysobulls, in the Roman Empire.—TRANS.

17   A firman was a royal mandate or decree issued by a sovereign in an Islamic state, primarily used in the Ottoman Empire. During various periods they were collected and applied as traditional bodies of law.—TRANS.

needed, either preemptively or repressively, to bring peace to the area. The privileges of Mount Athos do not need congressional ratification. This preferential form of government is autochthonous, self-sufficient, and perpetual. However, the current superiors were deceived, and they exchanged all of the above for a charter. Knowing all this, and feeling an inexpressible internal compulsion when the new charter was voted into common use, I felt that they were selling the inalienable rights of this sacred place. Oh, Elder Damascene, I saw the Holy Mountain dead and without governance from this new state of things, and for this reason I went over to the Protaton's bell tower and rang the bells in mourning, with the unwavering certainty that as of that day Mount Athos had ceased to exist as a self-ruling organism. The mournful bellringing interrupted the double Synaxis of the twenty monasteries, which was then in session, and they sent out the *Serdaris*[18] to find out who had died.

"He came to me and asked me who died, to which I replied, "Mount Athos," and continued to ring the bells. However, his gruff behavior forced me to stop, so I asked to be presented to the double Synaxis so we could perform the funeral service for the self-rule of Mount Athos.

"Unfortunately, the guards sent me away with the usual cursing and mocking, so I left, with great sadness in my heart. I tell you, Elder Damascene, when the echo of our old order of things can no longer be heard, and the rules and regulations of the new system are fully applied, this place will never again know peace. The true monastic culture will either be forced out, or it will be corrupted from abuses and the selling off of our priceless treasures and artefacts, which either the state or the bishop will find a way of taking advantage of."

These words are not those of a demon-possessed or insane man, but words of truth and wisdom.

---

18 During the Turkish occupation, the ruling Ottoman authorities created the position of Serdaris, who would be a Christian, and the only man allowed to have a weapon on Mount Athos. He would function as a guard and keeper of the peace, but since Mount Athos didn't need either very often, they came to maintain the roads and paths, act as guides for travelers and pilgrims, and serve as official escorts for visiting dignitaries or important events.—TRANS.

As we see in these stories, it seems Elder Kostas was not only not crazy but indeed very wise, as he knew many things, some of which were foreseen.

The community did not punish Kostas at the time, nor did they give much attention to his mournful ringing of the bells. Indeed, who would give any significance to the doings of "crazy-Kostas"? Many years later, however, in 1969, some "clever" men with worldly minds began to see Kostas around Karyes, and considered his appearance a disgrace, especially in light of the many Europeans who were coming to visit for the 1000-year celebration of Athos. So, they conspired and arranged to have the man of God sent to an asylum! There, examining him and finding him to be in perfect mental health, they sent him to a public home for the elderly, as Saint Païsius mentions. After that, all trace of him was lost.

The fathers who knew and understood him were greatly saddened, and always believed that "it was wrong, very wrong that they drove him away as they did, as he was not disruptive and did not bother anyone. He was an ornament and a precious gem for the Holy Mountain, not a disgrace." He was a fragrant flower in the all-beautiful garden of the Theotokos, the Holy Mountain. We, however, who see things with worldly eyes, treated him unjustly.

May we have his blessing. Amen.

Father Tikhon the Hermit

Papa-Tikhon, known in the world as Timothy, was born in the Russian town of Nova Mihaloshka in 1884, to Paul and Elena Golekov. He felt the monastic calling from the time when he was a child, and until he came of age he would travel to different monasteries in Russia as a pilgrim. He visited the Holy Land and after that came to Mount Athos, where he was tonsured at the cell of Saint Nicholas Bourazeris with the monastic name of Tikhon.

After five years there he felt a desire for a more intense spiritual life and went to Karoulia, where he stayed for fifteen years. He lived in a cave, ate once every three days, and spent his time in prayer, study, and prostrations. A wise and practical elder instructed and guided him during this time.

While he was living ascetically in Karoulia, he met two monks who fasted intensely, did a thousand prostrations a day, and died prematurely.

Later on, he moved to a cell belonging to the monastery of Stavronikita in Kapsala, living as a disciple of an elder for whom he cared until the elder died. After some encouragement, he became a priest and spiritual father and built a chapel which he dedicated to the feast of the Exaltation of the Holy Cross.

There was a time when two young monks came to be his disciples for a period of eight months. They were trying to follow his spiritual practices. He emphasized that they had all moved to the desert in order to live in a way that glorifies God, and not sleep and eat like animals. During the week they only ate food without oil, and that only once a day, while on Saturdays and Sundays he put three spoonfuls of oil in the food. Each one would then take his food and eat it alone in his cell. He would say, "You have a blessing to have seconds." He had discernment, and thus had *economia*[1] for his monks.

After their ascetic and oil-free meal, Father Tikhon would peacefully stroll around the area surrounding his hut, saying the Jesus prayer out loud in an ardent and heartfelt manner. It came out rhythmically, from the depths of his heart. When they asked him, "What are you doing, geronda?" he would answer: "The heart is just beginning to warm up."

He would pray unceasingly, even in his sleep; an incredible way of life. "I lie down, according to the needs of nature, but my heart remains awake, through the fullness of love."[2]

They spoke very little between themselves. At one point they went seventeen days without saying a word. Only when visitors came, he would call them to come and listen to the spiritual discussion and be benefited.

When old Nectarius "Karamanlis"[3] first went and visited him, he received him with love and set out a "proper dinner" for him. He went right then and gathered a handful of olives from a tree, and brought some sea salt and worm-infested rusks which he himself ate. Later he took leave of him, saying in his thick Russian accent, "Me now want to pray," and went into his cell. The visitor ate the food, as the possessionless ascetic offered it out of his love and simplicity.

---

1   The temporary deviation from the exactitude (akriveia) of the canons with the aim of greater spiritual benefit toward the salvation of the one concerned.—ED.
2   *The Ladder of Divine Ascent*, 30. 7
3   Historically, the Karamanlides (*sing* Karamanlis) were Turkish-speaking Orthodox Christians from the region of Cappadocia, who were driven out of their homes to Greece by the Treaty of Lausanne in 1923.—TRANS.

Father Tikhon blessing

The greatly pious shop owner of Karyes, Mr. Theodore Taleas, had Father Tikhon as a spiritual father. Once, when he had gone for confession, the previous visitor told him that Father Tikhon mentioned that "Theodore would be coming after him, and bringing this and that thing," which is exactly what happened.

Someone visited him, and Father Tikhon said, "You, my child, did not come for me, but to see if the area has wild boars."

For his monastic handiwork[4] he made epitaphios icons.[5] Sometimes a single icon took him two years two finish. In the beginning he worked on his handiwork for one hour a day, then for half an hour, and later on he stopped completely.

He carefully avoided judgment. When he would send his disciples to Karyes, he would walk with them for the first kilometer. During that walk they would pass by the hut of a Russian neighbor of theirs, a priest, who happened to be a little portly. In order that they not judge him for this, he paternally counseled them, "When you see Father E., you should say, 'This is a holy man! May we have his blessing!' and you should kiss his hand."

When they returned from Karyes, he would tell them not to bother him, but to just knock on the door of his cell so he would know that they were back, and after that to go to their cells. Once, from pious curiosity, one of them looked through the keyhole of his door to see what the elder was doing. He saw him weeping, wiping his tears with a kerchief, and lightly hitting his head with his hand. He loved repentance exceedingly, even though he led a holy life and was dedicated to God from his youth. His tears were his daily food. He had many tears and extreme compunction. With his tears he moistened the feet of the Crucified, and wiped them with his hair like the woman in the Scriptures. In his cell he worked spiritually, cultivating repentance and joyous mourning.

---

4   A monk's means of supporting himself and avoiding idleness.—TRANS.
5   The liturgical cloth depicting the deceased Christ and laid in the bier during the end of Holy Week and on the Holy Table during the Pascha season.—TRANS.

Whenever he heard confessions he was filled with compunction, and would weep with compassion for those confessing. One student of the Athoniada would confess to him, and later, after he became a priest, would say, "This bald head of mine has been soaked with the tears of Father Tikhon."

He usually celebrated the Divine Liturgy every Sunday, but he kept a portion of presanctified Host and would commune every day.

During the Divine Liturgy they would see his face transformed. His eyes, in the midst of the darkness, were radiant.

He always celebrated with compunction and tears. During the Divine Liturgy he read the Gospel with tears. He raised the Holy Host during the Great Entrance with tears, and all this aside, of course, from his spiritual raptures and divine visions.

When Father Tikhon was on his own, Elder Gerontius would help him celebrate liturgy. Father Tikhon paid him ten drachmas for every liturgy, at a time when priests usually received five drachmas.

Once, Elder Gerontius saw him lifted up above the ground, and from then on he would always say, "I haven't seen a greater saint on all of Athos."

Saint Païsius explained: "During the liturgy Father Tikhon would lock the church doors so that he would not be distracted. I would respond with 'Lord have mercy' from the hallway outside. Once, during the liturgy, at the moment of the sanctification of the Holy Gifts, his voice was lost. I waited for about five hours and did not interrupt, as I did not have a blessing to do so. After five hours he continued with 'Above all...'. Where was he for so many hours? Probably snatched up in spiritual contemplation. That day the Divine Liturgy finished in the afternoon."

He was completely without worldly cares and not interested in the least about worldly things. He never swept his cell, so the dirt and hair had made little piles on the floor, which looked like tortoiseshells.

He did about three thousand prostrations a day and counseled a certain monk: "You should do many prostrations, until your undershirt is soaked and you have to change it."

His feet were always swollen from the long hours of standing upright.

He fasted staunchly. One loaf of bread could last him an entire month. One day he sent two monks to gather fruit from the strawberry tree and boil it.[6] When he saw the water get red from the fruit, he told them that they should not cook this fruit again, as it bleeds too much.

He greatly loved studying spiritual writings. He would read for two or three hours and his soul was sweetened by it. He would say, "How sweet abba Isaac is!" He had read the complete works of Saint John Chrysostom two or three times.

All night he hardly slept. As soon as darkness fell, he would call the fathers to the church by hitting on the connecting wall between their cells. They prayed in church, and he chanted until the service of the Midnight Office. He would tell them to sit at certain times, and later on to stand again. They prayed for their benefactors and those who helped them, and afterwards went back to their cells. He told his monks, "You have my blessing to do as many prostrations as you want, and if you can, remain awake and pray all night long."

Father Tikhon said that in the monasteries there are monks who struggle and monks who are advanced in virtue. One of the latter is at Karakallou (Father Mathew), one at Iveron (Father Thanasis, who confessed to Father Tikhon), and one at Esphigmenou (another Father Thanasis).

The elder would say, "After three years' residence in a coenobium,[7] a monk is ready for spiritual warfare."

"Good habits are virtues, whereas bad habits are passions."

---

6   The strawberry tree is an evergreen shrub native to the Mediterranean region and western Europe. Despite the name, it is not closely related to the strawberry plant.—TRANS.

7   A monastery where monks live in a community rather than struggling alone.—TRANS.

"A monk should not have a relationship with animals, because these draw away his mind and heart. For instead of giving his love to God, it is distributed to the animals." He would mention that Saint Basil forbade the monk that would pet a cat or dog from communing.

"The Jesus prayer is like clean wheat. A good disciple can acquire the habit of unceasing prayer."

"If someone is careless with the study of the Holy Scriptures he can become deluded, like Origen."

"Three prostrations done with humility are better than a thousand done with high-mindedness."

"Only humility will save us. You will find very few truly humble people. You must search for them with a candle."

He loved humility so much that he went around all of Athos searching for a humble person. At last, in the monastery of Esphigmenou, he found a little elder who had wrapped himself in true and perfect humility as with a cloak. There were, of course, many others, but they were hidden from the eyes of most.

Once, the monastery of Esphigmenou invited Father Tikhon to confess the monks.[8] At that time there were more than sixty fathers. He had great reverence for Saint Anthony the Russian, and celebrated the Divine Liturgy in the cave where saint Anthony Pertseskaya lived. Then he returned to his cell by foot, walking quickly, despite the tiring day.

He had a deep friendship and wonderful relationship with Saint Silouan of the Russian Monastery, who, after passing away, appeared to Father Tikhon, and they spoke.

An elder of Karyes once said, "Father Tikhon was very simple and lived in his own world. He very violent,[9] spiritually, and despite fasting so much was strong in body. When he came to our cell and we gave him something to eat, he ate only two spoonfuls as a blessing. Today there is no one like him; don't even bother looking."

---

8   Many monks there were Russian-speaking.—TRANS.
9   Cf. Mt. 11:12: "the Kingdom of Heaven suffereth violence, and the violent take it by force."—ED.

One day he told his monks that when he dies, they should not move his body.[10] On hearing this, one of them thought: "I will move him and ask for his blessing [i.e. forgiveness] later." Father Tikhon, perceiving his thoughts, said: "You do not have a blessing." So, to this day, his venerable relics remain buried awaiting the general resurrection.

He fell asleep on the 10th of September 1968, after he saw a vision of the Virgin Mary with Saints Sergius and Seraphim, who told him that they would come and receive his soul after the feast of the Birth of the Mother of God.

His disciple, Elder Païsius, took care of him in his old age and was by him when he passed away. He buried him and inherited his cell. Afterwards, he wrote the life of Father Tikhon, who appeared to him after his death.

May we have his blessing. Amen.

---

10   It is a monastic habit that after three years a monk's remains are taken up and his bones reinterred in the ossuary of the monastery.—TRANS.

Elder Michael of Kafsokalyvia

Elder Michael, whose name in the world was Demetris G. Kalamias, was born on the island of Symi in the year 1906. His father was an organ-player by profession and also played bouzouki. When he was fifteen or sixteen years old, his father took him to Rhodes to buy him a bouzouki, so he could begin to work as a professional musician. During the return voyage, he traveled with a very devout Christian family. One of them saw the young man with the bouzouki, joyously enjoying it, and asked him, as though he did not know:

"What is that?"

"A bouzouki," answered the boy.

"You should know," the man then said, "that the number of strings a bouzouki has is the same number of demons it has on of it. When you play the bouzouki, the demons dance."

For the youth, this was a decisive moment. From that moment on he set aside the instrument and decided to become a monk. He did not even go to work anymore but prepared for the monastic life. His father kept saying, "At least work just enough so we can pay off the bouzouki." He, however, had made the great decision, and in the year 1922 left for the Holy Mountain.

He came and joined the brotherhood of Kafsokalyvia, in the cell of the Annunciation.

His elder's name was Arsenius, and he had come from another monastery outside of Athos. As he was virtuous and humble, worldly people visiting the monastery were constantly praising him, so, worrying and fearing lest he fall into pride from all the praise, he said to himself: "*Arsenie*, flee and be saved,"[1] and came to Athos.

For his handiwork Elder Arsenius made spoons, and was the cook for the community of Saint Joasaph. In this way, he and his disciple (whom after the period of novitiate he tonsured with the name Michael in the year 1923) got by. He taught Michael to make spoons as well, and the young monk made them very well, straight as a vigil candle, while his elder, who had poor eyesight, made them a bit crooked.

A certain pilgrim came to buy some spoons, and Father Michael gave him a few of the good ones he had made. The pilgrim, however, looked at them and said: "Do you have anything better?" At that moment, God enlightened Father Michael and he showed him the crooked ones his elder had made. The pilgrim was thrilled, exclaiming, "I want these!" and bought the crooked ones. Perhaps it was because they were made with prayer and had grace.

Father Michael was a very good disciple and ascetic. He was joined to Saint Porphyrius (who at that time was a monk in Kafsokalyvia) in friendship and brotherly love. They struggled together from the time they were novices. Their friendship was not a simple acquaintanceship, as Saint Porphyrius could clearly see the grace his companion had. For this reason, he asked that when he passed away they should bury him in the grave of Father Michael, and it happened just so.

At that time, an elder Theopemptos lived in the Skete of Kafsokalyvia. He lived a hesychastic life in a derelict cell at the edge of the Skete. He was violent,[2] a cultivater of noetic prayer, and a fool for Christ. The entire week he lived hesychastically, and on Sundays and feastdays he would go to liturgy and commune at the Kyriakon.[3]

---

1   As we read in the Sayings of the Desert Fathers, while the Great Arsenius was still employed in the imperial palace, he heard a voice say this to him, which was the occasion of his flight to the desert of Egypt.—ED.

2   See Matthew 11:12: "the kingdom Heaven suffereth violence, and the violent take it by force."—ED.

3   On Athos, the church where all the monks of a skete and monastic communities in a given area gather for Sunday services.—TRANS.

Elder Michael of Kafsokalyvia

Father Michael was joined with him in spiritual love. He provided the elder with dry bread and koumpania,[4] and the elder instructed him in noetic prayer. One day, Father Michael was spitting up blood and ran worried to Elder Theopemptos. The elder calmed him down saying that this was due to how forcefully he was reciting the Jesus prayer.

Father Michael greatly revered the Archangel Michael, not only because he was his namesake, but also because, as he himself told another monk in his community who had the same name, there was a time when he was doing his prayer rule and the Archangel Michael appeared to him and showed him how he should pray. The angel said, "Hold the prayer-rope like this, do the Jesus prayer like this, at the same time cross yourself and make small prostrations."

As time went on, Athonite spoons began to go out of fashion, so Father Michael learned to paint icons. When his elder passed away, Father Gabriel, who came to be his disciple, taught him the art of iconography. Father Michael was a good iconographer, and he would compose the icons with prayer and reverence, and for this reason miracles sometimes occurred.

Father Gabriel explained: "There was a time when my elder Michael was painting an icon of Christ. He then saw Christ in his sleep, and Christ told him that He was pleased, and that the icon was beautiful, only there was a small detail that needed correcting."

Father Michael also made an icon of the Archangel Michael, just as he had seen him in the vision.

At that time, Saint Nectarius had appeared in the island of Rhodes to a farmer that was going to Archipolis and told him to build a church. Indeed, a beautiful church was built, and they ordered an icon of the saint from Elder Michael. This icon performed many miracles, both then and now. At one point they brought a paralyzed Turk to venerate it, who then left healed.

He also painted the icon of Saint Savvas of Kalymnos. When they brought the icon to Kalymnos, the bells started ringing on their own.

---

4   A Cretan dessert.—TRANS.

Once, two fathers from Saint Basil's visited him. While they were speaking together and Elder Michael was writing an icon, tears started to flow like a river and his face turned red. The fathers were worried and asked him what happened. He calmed them, telling them that the tears come from the power of the noetic prayer, which he was trying to say unceasingly. Whenever he wanted, he could begin crying. When people asked him, he would speak to them about noetic prayer. He himself was helped by Elder Theopemptos and by another elder who lived ascetically on the small, dry island of Saint Christopher, across from Kafsokalyvia.

When he became old and sick, his disciple put a zipper on his blanket so that he would not accidenatally uncover himself at night and get cold. One night he heard a conversation in the cell of Elder Michael. He opened the door to see with whom he was speaking, and Elder Michael said to him, "What have you done to me! Saint Nectarius came, and I could not get up."

Elder Michael knew where the relics of Saint Maximos of Kafsokalyvia were buried, and he told his friend Elder Porphyrius.

As all who knew him would later relate, Elder Michael was a virtuous monk and a man of God, blameless like a little lamb. He loved the church services. He did not perform any great ascetic feats, or particular fasts or vigils. He was, however, extremely merciful, meek, and peaceful towards all. He had a great love for all the other fathers. He would leave his own work and go to help any who were sick and in need. He took in and cared for the elderly Father Athanasios Strezova the spiritual father and hesychast, the last successor of the brotherhood of Father Chariton.

He had the grace of helping and comforting young monks by telling wonderful stories. For example, he would say about pride, "A proud man would prefer to climb to the peak of Athos three times rather than say, 'Bless [i.e. forgive] me'." He gave excellent and practical counsel to the pilgrims that passed by his cell. He told one priest who preached well, "You should speak out. Do you not see how many people the communists have led astray with their insistent and continuous preaching?"

He was pious and loved by all the fathers and fell asleep peacefully in the year 1978.

May we have his blessing. Amen.

Elder Theophilos of the Great Lavra

He was born in the village of Kaniani in Lamia in the year 1885. He was baptized Thomas (with the surname of Kapsis), and came to the Great Lavra to become a monk on the 14th of July, 1910. After a one-year novitiate, he was tonsured on the 15th of July, receiving the name Theophilos.

Father Theophilos, though living in an idiorhythmic monastery,[1] struggled greatly towards spiritual excellence and was very ascetic. He was a man of prayer and monastic exactness and never missed a church service. He entered his *stasidi*[2], always standing throughout the service, and would never sit or leave it until the service was finished.

He wanted the services to follow the proper order, and when he saw irregularities he went up and corrected them. There was a time when a young monk began to chant the Polyeleos pompously and in a stylized manner during the vigil. After the first verse, Elder Theophilos went up and told him: "Neither God nor men are listening to you. The demons are dancing. We should chant humbly; humbly, so that God may hear us and rejoice in us as His children."

---

1   A monastery where each monk sets his own schedule and has his own savings, gathering with the others only for services, as opposed to cenobitic monasticism where monks live communally.—ED.

2   Booths filling the walls of the inside of a church where attendees can stand or sit. —TRANS.

Elder Theophilos of Lavra
(This picture is from the book of Chrysostom, Bishop of Rodostolon,
Longing and Grace on Athos.)

In order to practice greater asceticism, he never lit a fire in the winter when he was alone in his cell, and he never wore the thick woolen stockings common in the winter at that time.

He fasted a great deal, and the heads of the monastery gave him a more lenient fasting rule to tone down the extremity of his fasting so that he would not die. He would not eat before his self-appointed eating time, as he considered it secret eating.[3] He gathered fruit, put it into his kerchief, and did not eat a single one until that pre-appointed eating time. When that time came, he would pray over the food and then eat. He never ate meat, even though he lived in an idiorhythmic monastery.

The Great Lavra annually gave a small amount of money to all the monks of the community for their needs. Elder Theophilos did not use it for himself but rather donated it back to the Lavra for the repair of the monastery's oven. He lived in such poverty and simplicity that he did not have needs and expenses.

He initially served as sacristan and in later years as the cellarer. On January 15, 1935, he was selected as the *proistamenos*,[4] but he resigned shortly thereafter, as the management, contact with officials, and necessary worldly cares that the position required clashed with his personality and ascetic way of life.

There was a time, during the years that he served as cellarer, when he lost the keys. Since his eyesight was poor, he called Father Basil and they searched the grounds, all the way to the garden. Not finding them, Elder Theophilos said: "We have done what is humanly possible. Now I'll pray on my prayer-rope for Saint Menas to find them." He went to his cell, lit a candle, and began praying. Before he even finished his first prayer-rope, the keys fell in front of him.

---

3   I.e., eating outside of the ordained times, without a blessing, in one's cell.—ED.

4   An administrative position.—TRANS.

During Bright Week one year he went to Karyes with Father Basil to visit two monks, Father Arethas and Father Kosmas. The fathers opened the door but did not say a word. First they chanted "Christ is Risen" and other hymns, and afterward they welcomed the visitors and spoke with them, as the fathers did in the old days.

Everyone at Great Lavra respected Elder Theophilos for his virtues, and many young men who came to become monks had him as their spiritual father.

He was beloved by all, as he was peace-loving and virtuous. Once, he heard two monks quarrelling. He immediately went and told them: "Both of you are to blame. You should each do a prostration to the other and forgive each other." They listened to him, did what he told them, and felt peace.

One time while praying he came to spiritual contemplation and saw a vision. Afterwards he told Father Basil: "I was shocked by the things I saw, but I cannot tell anyone what they were."

In the summer of 1964, after the millennial celebrations, the Great Lavra decided to allow a boat with female pilgrims to come near the port, though not to touch the Holy Mountain itself, and to have priests take a piece of the Holy Cross and some relics onboard for a few minutes so that the pilgrims might venerate them. When Elder Theophilos learned of this he was troubled, as he considered it unfitting and not according to tradition. He approached the Synaxis of the Monastery and tried with many arguments to convince them to cancel the trip. When he failed to convince them, he exhorted the monks whom he counseled to pray the prayer-rope all night. The boat had arrived in the harbor already, the sea was as smooth as oil, and the veneration of the relics would be the next day. However, that night, the prayers of Elder Theophilos and the other fathers brought about a change in weather, a storm arose, and the boat left to find a safer harbor.

There was a time when Elder Theophilos fell ill, and Father Basil took him to the hospital. There, they pleaded with him to eat some meat for nourishment now that he was sick, but he refused saying, "So many years on Mount Athos, I did not eat meat, and I'll eat it now?" He would not even eat yogurt on fasting days. Later, they brought him back to Lavra in a wheelchair. He remained bedridden in his cell. One morning, six priests came to perform the service of Holy Unction; by the afternoon he had gotten up and out of bed. The fathers were puzzled as to how he had recovered so quickly. When Father Basil asked him, Elder Theophilos answered innocently, "Why did you perform Holy Unction? Did you not do it so I would become well? You should have reverence and faith in the sacraments."

From that day, he lived another ten years in perfect health. In 1978, on Great and Holy Monday, he went around all the cells asking all the fathers for forgiveness. On Holy Tuesday he did not come down to the service. On Holy Wednesday he called Father Basil before dawn and asked him to come and commune him, because in two hours he would be gone. Father Basil did as he asked, and in exactly two hours the elder handed his sanctified soul to the Lord, Whom he had worshiped and served all his life.

He fell asleep and was entombed on Great and Holy Wednesday, the 18th of April, 1978. He was 93 years old.

May we have his blessing. Amen.

Father Methodius of Karyes

Father Methodius was a Romanian by descent. He was born in Sibiu, on December 26, 1905, to John and Evdokia Popa. At his baptism he was given the name Basil. He came to Mount Athos to become a monk and became a part of the monastic community of Koutloumousi, living at the cells of the two Saint Theodores.[1] He was tonsured in April of 1932 and took the name Methodius. On account of his purity and piety they ordained him a priest.

One day his elder sent him to the monastery of Esphigmenou to give them some of the handiwork the two of them had made, leaving him with the express command to return on the same day. By the time he completed the task, the weather had turned and rain began to pour. The fathers at Esphigmenou tried to prevent him from leaving in such weather, but having his elder's command in mind he began on his homeward journey, albeit with great difficulty. After a while, however, finding it impossible to continue, he found a hollow tree trunk, squeezed inside, and began praying. He fell asleep, momentarily, and when he woke up, he saw a light nearby outside. He thought: "I'll go and knock for help." He went, knocked, and found out that it was his own cell. His elder, who had anxiously been waiting for him, was awestruck, and marveled at his obedience.

In later years, after his elder fell asleep, he moved to the cell of the two Saint Theodores in Karyes, which belongs to the community of Saint Paul, and lived ascetically, with spiritual integrity and self-denial.

---

1 St. Theodore the Tyro and St. Theodore the Commander. —TRANS.

Father Methodius was virtuous, and this was evident from his simplicity, his peacefulness, his humility, his many virtues, and his blameless life. He loved the church services and struggled towards ever greater spiritual heights. He did not neglect the services and his spiritual work. The fathers remember that even in his old age he wore his cassock and did his prayer rule.

He was a humble man with much love. He offered hospitality to a certain pious and virtuous layman named Kostas. When Kostas fell asleep in the Lord, his body did not stiffen. He was granted the gift of post-mortem flexibility, which is seen in some monks. Indeed, some believed that he was a secret monk.

There was a time when a *kaviotis* lived in his cell, and this monk suffered from the passion of the love of money. He gathered the money he made, turned it to gold liras, put them in a metal canister, buried the canister, and piled animal manure and used food tins on top of the hole in order for the location to remain secret. At one point Father Methodius had gone to the feast of Saint George Phaneromenos, and the same night his cell caught on fire. One part of the structure burned, but they arrived in time to save the other part. Unfortunately, the money-loving *kaviotis* was found inside, dead. When Father Methodius began to clear out the burned part of the structure and throw out whatever was damaged by the fire, he found the metal canister with the liras. Grieved, he kicked the canister, and the room filled with liras. "My, my" he said, "a devil. This is why the house burned. Whoever wants them, let him take them. I'm not keeping any." Two fathers took some of the liras, and later on became sick and suffered greatly.

One year, on Saint Paul's feastday, there was a storm, and they had pulled the wooden boat they used to come and go from their cell onto the dock. After the feast, ten to fifteen people tried to push it back into the sea and they could not. At that point, Father Methodius told them to move aside a little, and he pulled it back into the water on his own, not with his own strength but with the strength God gave him, as he had prayed for it.

He would narrate a shocking event that happened in Romania: "A monk from the neighboring village abandoned the monastic

Father Methodius of Karyes

schema and got married. The years passed, he had children, and eventually the time came for his death. They prepared the body and asked a priest to come at a certain time for the funeral service. The priest did as he was asked and went to perform the funeral service. When he got there, however, he saw the house empty; no one was there. He went to the second floor and saw only the coffin. He was perplexed and wondered what was happening. At that point he heard heavy footsteps on the stairs, and turning he saw a large bear in front of him. The bear spoke to him saying: "Why did you come to do a service for him? He was a monk and rejected his schema. Do as much praying as you want: this one is mine!", and immediately the bear took the remains and disappeared. At that moment, the priest's eyes were opened and he saw the throng of people who were in the room mourning for the deceased man. He was stunned and in a daze, and when he came to, he asked that they take him home. He did not perform the funeral service. Once he had fully recovered, he explained all the shocking things he had seen to his relatives, and, after requesting and receiving permission from his wife, he moved to Mount Athos, where he lived the rest of his days in asceticism and repentance."

Father Methodius knew this priest personally and had heard the story from his own lips, so he emphatically shared it with others.

People would ask Father Methodius why he would not accept a disciple, and he would answer: "Romanians have just now begun to come to Mount Athos, but these are the children of Communism. In my day, we did things differently."

The monks of Saint Paul's loved Father Methodius, and every time they went to Karyes they stayed in his cell overnight. When he got old, they pleaded with him to allow them to take him to the monastery and care for him in his old age. On the one hand he was willing, but he was afraid that they would make him a spiritual father, as they had done with Father Macarius from Lakkou Skete, to whom many Romanians from all over Mount Athos went for confession.[1] Father Methodius considered himself unworthy; he

---

1   At that time there were not many Romanian-speaking spiritual fathers on Athos, so more were always needed for the Romanian pilgrims and monks. —TRANS.

feared the responsibility and would say: "I am not for such things. It is too great a responsibility for me. I won't be able to figure it out."

Father Methodius got sick during Great Lent in 1979. Saint Païsius tells us[2] that on the Sunday of the veneration of the Holy Cross he called his fellow Romanian Father Christopher and sent him to inform their compatriot Father Joachim (who at the time was being cared for in old age at Koutloumousiou) that this time tomorrow they would die together. He also asked his forgiveness for whatever shortcomings he exhibited in his behavior towards him. Father Joachim believed Father Methodius and prepared himself joyously, praying to the Panagia while awaiting the hour of his repose. The next day at five (in Byzantine time, which is the time observed on Mount Athos) Father Joachim fell asleep peacefully at the same time as Father Methodius, just as the latter had foreknown and predicted. It was the 13th of March, 1979. The two sanctified souls left for heaven together. They were like brothers in life, and had great love between them. They had asked of God that they not be separated in this life or in the next, and so it happened.

May we have his blessing. Amen.

---

2   "Ἁγιορεῖτες Πατέρες καὶ Ἁγιορείτικα ˆAthonite Fathers and Athonite Matters,"] 2nd ed. 1993, p. 108-109

The neptic Auxentius of Grigoriou

The Watchful Auxentius of Grigoriou

He was born in 1893 in Mandra,[1] to Constantine and Evangelia Konstanoni. He was an Arvanitis.[2] By ancient descent his ancestors were from the land of martyrs, the long-suffering Northern Epirus.[3] When he was baptized, they named him Athanasius. He was the firstborn, and his parents had three more boys and two girls, one of which, Antigone, also became a nun taking the name Anysia. When Athanasius was an infant he did not breastfeed on Wednesdays and Fridays, just like Saint Nicholas; this was a foreshadowing of his later lifelong self-control.

He loved the church and prayer, and the younger children marveled at his goodness. While growing up he helped his father with farming and cattle-rearing.

There was a cave near their village, and every night a light appeared there; for this reason the whole area came to be called Candili.[4] The cave was in a precipitous crag, very high up, and no one had managed to climb to it successfully. Athanasius, however, made the dangerous climb and stayed two days and nights in the cave. A divine event transpired during his stay, which greatly influenced

1   Also known as Kountoura. A village in the region of Elefsina, in Greece. — TRANS.
2   A Christian, bilingual population group in Greece who traditionally speak Arvanitika, an Albanian language variety, along with Greek. They moved from Southern Albania and settled in Greece during the Middle Ages, primarily to avoid the Ottoman islamization of the country. Arvanites self-identify as Greek and do not consider themselves Albanian, a term which they consider an insult. —TRANS.
3   An area that spans the border of modern day Greece and Albania.—TRANS.
4   "Candle", i.e. a votive lamp.—ED.

him. When he returned, without saying a word to anyone, he left for the monastery of Penteli, planning to become a monk. He did not stay there long, however, moving instead to the monastery of Saint Meletius and becoming a novice. During that time, however, he was drafted and served in the army during the war in Asia Minor. After two years he was discharged, and in 1920 he came to Mount Athos, to the Monastery of Grigoriou, to become a monk. He was 28 years old.

His willingness in service, his exactness in obedience, his dutifulness in monastic life, his spiritual struggle, and his love of God made an impression on the fathers and in only year he was tonsured a monk of the great schema.

He served at the church, in the mill, in the kitchen, in the gardens, and even in the dependencies [metochia]. He was compassionate, industrious, and attentive in his service. He wore himself out constantly, and for the first eleven years of his monastic life he battled with sleepiness. He was saddened by this, as sometimes after laboring all day sleep would overtake him during the evening service. He confessed it to his abbot, Father Thanasis, who reassured him: "Monastery church services are like a boat that is traveling: one will hold vigil, another sleeps, then they switch, and the boat continues. They will, indeed, arrive at their destination." Father Auxentius was strengthened, took courage, continued his struggle, and eventually conquered his sleepiness. In this way he managed even to keep vigil in his cell for the whole night, either by sitting on a specific chair, or by doing full and small prostrations, crossing himself and praying on his prayer-rope. He rested a little during the day. This continued into his later years when he lost his sight and suffered from a hernia.

The abbot had appointed a monk to keep vigil each night, going around as a night watchman, checking if any of the monks needed any assistance. Every time he checked on the blind Elder Auxentius, the elder was always upright in prayer. As soon as he would hear the watchman, however, he would quickly lay on his bed and pretend to be asleep . The fathers who learned about this would sometimes come and enter his cell noiselessly, as to not interrupt him or be perceived, and they always saw him upright in prayer.

Elder Auxentius was a quiet monk and a lover of peace. When he saw scandals, he immediately fled. His spoke very little, pouring his energy into his ascetic struggles instead. He avoided discussions, because as he would say, "When I speak, I afterwards have trouble in my spiritual labors, as I get distracted by other thoughts."[5] He did not even crave company and conversation when he got old, as usually happens with the elderly. He preferred silence and *hesychia* so that his noetic work would not be interrupted, and when younger monks came to his cell and overstayed their welcome, he would simply stop talking completely, thereby giving them to understand that they must now leave him alone. There was a time when the monk appointed to take him to and from the services was trying to spark up a conversation on the way back to his cell. Elder Auxentius cut him off sternly: "Do not speak to me while we walk." He did not want anyone to take his mind away from prayer. He was a monk of actions, but also of spiritual contemplation. He was, essentially, a practicer of watchfulness[6] (nepsis) living in community. He was of such great spiritual stature that it would be difficult to find another like him, even in the desert. As long as he lived in this world, until his death, he did not cease his noetic prayer. For this reason he remained closed in his cell, not going about outside and avoiding conversation, lest he interrupt his noetic prayer.

He counseled: "You should be saying the Jesus prayer continually, as in this way you will be united with Christ. By the Jesus prayer one feels union with God. You must understand that God is everything. Drive away tempting thoughts through the Jesus prayer. Christ Himself will teach you and enlighten you; only make sure that your mind is inside your heart and not focused on the world. When you

5   See the magazine Ὁ Ὅσιος Γρηγόριος, vol. 6 (1981), p. 95. Of the many beautiful things written there by Elder George and the fathers of Grigoriou Monastery about Elder Auxentiu, we are using some elements, with their blessing, so as to complete his synaxarion.

6   Watchful (nepticos): A word describing an Orthodox theology of asceticism which includes unceasing prayer, constant ascetical struggle, sobriety in all things, persistent and true repentance, and the perpetual cleansing of one's soul to achieve perfection in holiness. —TRANS.

are tired, you should say the Jesus prayer out loud, as your mind may tire and wander, but your senses will bring you back if you stop. All I have to say to you is 'Lord Jesus Christ Have Mercy on Me'; that is my counsel; nothing else."[7]

When they asked him, "What must we do to gain the Kingdom of Heaven?", he would answer, "We should continuously say 'Lord Jesus Christ, have mercy on me'." He recommended the Jesus prayer to all, telling them to have it in their heart. When laymen asked for counsel, he would tell them keep the commandments and read the Holy Scriptures.

He himself had acquired the gift of unceasing prayer, and indeed was at such an advanced spiritual state that he would say the Jesus prayer even in his sleep, as he revealed to Saint Paisios in his unutterably simple manner.

Another time he told him: "I am blind, as you see, but when I say the Jesus prayer or do my prayer rule with my prayer-rope I often see a light on my right hand side. It leaves and comes back. But the most important thing is the love for Christ that the prayer brings to the heart."

He saw the Uncreated Light, and one day, not seeing it, he was concerned and asked his spiritual father if he could go to confession.

Once, Elder Auxentius went to commune in the chapel of Saint Gregory the Founder, where they were celebrating the Divine Liturgy. Having prepared, he approached the chalice with great joy and piety. The celebrant priest, however, was blinded by a strong and radiant light that was emanating from Elder Auxentius' face. His face was completely covered. It practically disappeared in that bright sun, brighter than the actual radiance of the sun, and the priest not only could not commune him but could not even look at him. He looked away, and later explained, "His face was shone so brightly that when I looked, I got dizzy and nearly fell down. I put my hand over my eyes because I could not bear the brightness. He was shining from top to bottom." When after a little while the Uncreated Light subsided and

7   See the magazine Ὁ Ὅσιος Γρηγόριος, vol. 6 (1981),p. 95-96.

the surprised priest came to himself, then he was able to commune him.

Elder Auxentius frequently saw the Uncreated Light and had arrived at the state of Divine Eros; and all this from his persistence in prayer.

He had also learned many other prayers by heart, and he would alternate them with the Jesus prayer. He knew the entire Akathist Hymn, including the Canon, and chanted it often. Every night he would recite the Psalter from memory. He had memorized it, and prayed both it and the Jesus prayer continuously. He loved the services very much. He particularly liked the prayers for Holy Communion and read them ardently. He did not want to miss a word from any service, so sometimes, when he could not hear well, he would move closer to the reader and other times he would shout, "Louder!"

Elder Auxentius held to his monastic vow of poverty: he was extremely poor. He had nothing, and he did not desire anything in this life except Christ. He did not wear new clothes, and during his entire monastic life he only used one pair of shoes. On the road, when no one was watching, he put them under his arm and walked barefoot. He did this for ascesis, to discipline his body, but also because he did not want to ruin the shoes. Once, when he was absent from his cell, the monks were cleaning and threw away some of his decayed and seemingly unusable undershirts. When he found out, he was distraught. He climbed down over the cliff where they had thrown them and picked them up again. He had nothing in his cell except some icons and a few books.

He was completely detached from the world and had no communication with any of his biological relatives. When, after thirty years, his siblings came to see him, he fled into the vineyards to avoid them. Only when the fathers insisted that he speak to his siblings, in order to be obedient he spoke to them, telling them not to bother him again.

As his fellow monastics all bear witness, Father Auxentius was very violent.[8] He wore himself out serving others; he dug in the vineyards and fasted strictly. He was an ascetic and completely unaware

8   See Matthew 11:12: "the kingdom Heaven suffereth violence, and the violent take it by force."—ED.

of certain kinds of food. When he was sick in his old age, the monk who was taking care of him asked him if he would prefer halva or jam. Confused, he asked: "What is jam?"

The cook and the cook's assistant had the task of taking food to Elder Auxentius. One day they saw him coming to the kitchen. When he got there, he asked: "Give me a little food if you don't mind. I haven't eaten for three days." Then, realizing they had forgotten to bring him food for the last three days, they made a prostration and apologized. He did not complain or protest to anyone.

He had great self-denial. He remained blind rather than going out into the world to have his eyes operated on. He did not have surgery for his hernia, despite all the pain and suffering. He did not want to have other people's teeth in his mouth; so, when all his teeth fell out, he insisted on remaining toothless. He had trouble with hard food but did not want anyone to be put out of his way or make food particularly for him. When they would ask him what he wanted to eat, the answer was always the same: "Whatever everyone else is having." He always ate in a measured manner and with self-control. If anyone tried to pressure him to eat more, he would say, "Do not pressure me. Large amounts of food are not well-pleasing to God." Whenever a monk would bring him his meal, he would give that monk part of the food he was bringing.

When he received communion, he would close himself in his cell and pray. He did not speak to anyone and would not answer the door. Once, after Holy Communion, the fathers found him prostrate in his cell praying. He was taken up with contemplation and did not perceive the fathers observing him.

Being blind and having poor hearing he would lose track of time, and not wanting to miss the service he would usually set out from his cell for the church two hours ahead of time. One night he tripped and fell, injuring himself, soaking his cassock with the blood that was running from his nose. He was exhausted and could not get up. They found him after two hours, covered in blood and nearly frozen, and brought him to the geriatric care ward of the monastery. There they cleaned him up, and a monk stayed behind to take care of him. When he perceived that the fathers left, thinking he was alone, he threw off the covers, stood up and began to do his prayer rule, going for hours on the prayer-rope. The fathers would say to him: "Now you are an old man. Remain in your cell. You do not need to come to the services." He replied: "Do not deprive me of the church. It is only there that I feel authentic freedom."

Before he lost his sight he read the *Philokalia* in its original Greek. He read the entire five volumes four times. When the fathers asked him what they should read, he would always recommend the *Philokalia*. And when they told him that they did not understand it, he would answer, "It's alright. You'll start to understand it gradually."

He had a special love for the *Philokalia*, because he himself was a great practicer of watchfulness with similar experiences as those he read about in his beloved Philokalic fathers. As he confessed to his spiritual father, on the twelfth prayer-rope of his prayer rule he saw the Uncreated Light, though he was completely blind. And even though he had the gift of unceasing prayer and did one hundred and fifty full prostrations a day even in his old age, he would still humble himself saying, "I am walking in the dark, callousness has a hold on me, and I live in vanity."

Once, Father Isaac of Kapsala visited him and asked: "How do we know when the Jesus prayer has truly moved to our heart?" The elder answered: "When the worldly thoughts cease." Father Isaac then asked him to tell him about great things that will happen in the world, about the Uncreated Light, about his visions, and how to be able to achieve them. To this, the elder answered sharply, saying: "Do not seek such things. You should be seeking purification from the passions."

Once, two young men prostrated themselves before him and asked for his blessing to become novices. He prayed over them and counseled them: "May you proceed on the path of true repentance."

Elder Auxentius, struggling with old age and illnesses, showed great patience, having his beloved Jesus prayer as an inseparable companion. It was in this victorious manner that he arrived at the end of his monastic journey. He was obedient even unto death, violent even unto blood,[9] possessionless in the extreme, estranged from the world, a friend of God, beloved and esteemed by his fellow monks, a standard of monastic exactness, and great practicer of watchfulness, accomplished in unceasing prayer.

He fell asleep in the Lord on March 1st, 1981, at the age of 89, on the dawn of the Sunday of Orthodoxy, fully prepared for the next life. The abbot and fathers spoke with wonder of Elder Auxentius, being moved by his ascetic accomplishments, and they felt that they were sending forth a holy man to the Church of the Firstborn in the Kingdom of Heaven.

After his falling asleep, a brother asked Saint Païsius if Elder Auxentius had been saved. The saint replied, "If he was not saved, then none of us will be saved."

His venerable skull emits a sweet aroma at times, which some fathers are able to perceive.

May we have his blessing. Amen.

---

9   See Matthew 11:12: "the kingdom Heaven suffereth violence, and the violent take it by force."—ED.

Elder Arsenius of Simonopetra

Elder Arsenius of Simonopetra

His family was from Epirus by descent, but he himself was born in 1913 in Fortosa, a village near Ioanina. His parents, Demetriss and Chrysavgi were of the lower social class and poor but faithful and pious. They baptized him, giving him the name Nicholas, and raised him with the simple, traditional piety of the countryside. He received little formal education, instead helping his parents in various jobs around the house. When he was a child, he had an accident and suddenly found himself under the feet of a young bull. He spontaneously called out to the Panagia for help, and the bull passed over him without hurting a hair on his head. From that moment on he considered our Panagia his protector.

Nicholas left his village while still young and went to Athens to live with his uncle who owned a bakery. From the break of dawn, Nicholas and his uncle were in the bakery, kneading bread and *koulouria*.[1] When they were done, Nicholas would take a tray of *koulouria* and go out into the street early in the morning to sell them to workers and passers-by.

Archimandrite Ieronymos, then the abbot of Simonopetra, a very virtuous and spiritual man, saw him one day on a street corner. When the young boy asked him if he wanted a *koulouri*, he jokingly replied "I want you, not the *koulouri*," and bought a *koulouri*. Discerning the child's deep longings, he spoke to him about Mount Athos, about our

---

1   A sesame-seed-covered bread in the shape of a large ring, larger but thinner than a bagel, traditionally served as a cheap Greek street food. It was, and still is today, sold early in the morning in bakeries and by street vendors in highly frequented areas.—TRANS.

Panagia, about the saints, the ascetics, the monks, and Simonopetra. In this way he lit a new fire inside the young boy's heart, which Nicholas preserved through his later meetings with the holy elder, when the elder would come to Athens to confess his spiritual children and stayed at the dependency of Simonopetra, located in the Analipsis Vyronos area.

Every monastic calling begins wondrously and in a manner specific to the particular human soul. In this case, the words and example of Elder Ieronymos caused the young child to think about monasticism and dedication to God. He thought about these things, cultivated them, and when they had matured, he decided to actualize his intention to leave the world, go to Mount Athos, and become a monk and ascetic.

He found a way and made it to Thessaloniki, and from there by foot to Mount Athos. It was a three-day journey. However, in order to enter Mount Athos as a novice one had to have the necessary paperwork: a birth certificate, identity card, et cetera. He did not have any of that, and since he was still a child the authorities did not let him enter. Men from Epirus, however, are known for their toughness, bravery, and fearlessness, and so he circled the peninsula by foot and entered through the northern side of Athos, which had no guards. He arrived at Simonopetra in 1929, where he was received by Elder Ieronymos.

At that time, however, the accursed practice of provincialism was prevalent on the Holy Mountain, and each monastery had monks only from a specific geographic area.[2] If someone from another region went to become a monk, they would turn him away, even if they needed him, or, even if they kept him temporarily, they would force him to leave on his own through humiliation and derisive words and actions. This is what happened in the case of Elder Arsenius.

The monastery, on account of the calendar issue,[3] went through a deep and—for them—earth-shattering crisis, and as a result of

2   There was a monastery for Russians, a monastery for men from Asia Minor, a monastery for Northern Greeks, etc. —TRANS.
3   Referring to when the Church of Greece moved from the traditional Julian Calendar to the Gregorian calendar during the first part of the twentieth centu-

that they removed the abbot Ieronymos from his position, despite his spirituality and essential contribution to the reinvigoration of the monastery. At that time, he was exiled to the monastery of Koutlou-mousiou and from there to the dependency of the Ascension. His monastic spiritual children who were not from Asia Minor were also sent away from the monastery. Father Arsenius, who at that time was still a young monk, ended up in Kafsokalyvia, in the cell of the Annunciation, in obedience to Elder Michael, moving there after he heard that there were holy monks and ascetics in the area.

Life in an Athonite skete is rough and laborious. A monk has to do the majority of the work on his own, and if the entire brotherhood consists of only a few people, the younger monks bear most of the burden: daily services, personal prayer rules, errands, problems, issues, serving the more elderly fathers, and doing the monastic handiwork in order to make a living.

In Father Arsenius' cell[4] they made wooden spoons. He learned the craft easily, but the more he learned and worked at it, the more the flame of asceticism slowly extinguished inside him. So he hid that ascetic spark, waiting for better days. Father Arsenius lived there from 1930 to 1941, working, living in obedience, and becoming sanctified.

The brutal war of 1940[5] and the resulting lack of basic necessities and mass starvation caused the monks to no longer be able to live by selling handiwork, and forced the ascetics to go to the monasteries in search of their "daily bread." Amidst the evils of the war, God bless-ed the olive harvest that year, and the trees had a particularly large yield. The ascetics came to the monasteries and were given parts of the olive groves to harvest, working 50/50 (they would keep half and the monastery would keep half). So, after ten years, Father Arsenius found himself at his beloved Simonopetra once again. He worked for the season, and when the olive harvest ended, he asked to stay

---

ry. This innovation led to schisms and a loss of cohesion among the Church in Greece.—TRANS.

4   A cell (*kelli*) is either a monk's own room in a monastery or an independent house where lives an elder with or without disciples. Here the latter is meant.—ED.

5   World War II. —TRANS.

for good, remembering that it was there that he started his monastic life, and he always considered it his place of repentance. The older fathers who had originally sent them away had departed for heaven, one after the other, and to his great joy the monks who remained were relieved to have him stay, as the needs were great and the monks few.

But again, the internal situation of the monastery during this time was not good. Abbot Caesarius had left the monastery on account of the Germans, and Simonopetra was going through difficult times. Despite these things, Father Arsenius went through many positions. He served in the church, the guesthouse, the dining hall, and the port, Daphne. He worked wherever he was needed willingly, yet, as he would say, without spiritual ascesis and deep contemplation. "Let today be today. God will provide for tomorrow." The spark of asceticism, for which reason he first became a monk, was deeply covered in the ash of distraction over daily cares and in danger of being extinguished entirely. And so, amidst all the confusion and disorder, God showed him His presence and providence with certain signs and reminded him of His hope of a return to the first purpose of his monasticism. Or, in his own words, "*Arsenie*, this is the reason you left the world."[6]

He served at the monastery's port, and one day decided to go fishing. At one point he felt the boat running adrift and not yielding to his efforts to maneuver it. The current of the sea swept him away, and he was being pushed farther and farther away from land. Night fell, and he lost all contact with Athos. He then turned with tears to his protectress, the Theotokos, and to Saint Nicholas, for whom there was a chapel at the port, whose vigil candles he lit daily. He asked for their help, and suddenly he found himself and his boat in the port, not that of his own monastery but that of Daphne.

The years passed and he continued to live with complete spiritual indifference: "I did not even fulfill the basic monastic practices," he would say. In order to move forward in the monastic life, one needs continuous encouragement through examples, words, and effort. Just as a fire will go out if it has nothing to feed on, so it goes with monas-

---

6   Or "[bear in mind] for what you came out." This is what Saint Arsenius the Great would say to himself, according to the Sayings of the Desert Fathers.—ED.

ticism. If the activities of spirituality are absent, then indifference, listlessness, spiritual paralysis, and death will reign.

He explained his departure from spiritual indifference and his integration into the monastic program in the following way. It happened in a miraculous fashion, according to the concession of God. God knew the depths of his soul and did not want him to be lost; and so, He arranged for his change of life.

"I was steward at Daphne. We had a lot of workers back then, as Germany had not yet opened its borders to Greeks.[7] They did not require a lot to work. I planted gardens and bred chickens, which resulted in a plethora of eggs and cockerels; I then sold them, and with the money I earned I paid the workers and then had golden crowns made for my teeth."

Gold was dentists' material of choice at that time, so that problematic teeth would not completely rot.

"No ascetic life at all. From the easy living, "I grew fat... and forsook the Beloved."[8] After this they asked me to take on the service of *trapezaris*.[9] Again, very little to do. There were not many monks there. Much free time. Idleness is the mother of all vice. I remembered that when I was a child in the village, I used to catch birds in traps. Passions and weaknesses love to come around again. And so I tried it again, and one day I caught two or three wild doves. I boiled them. Every monk in the monastery was allowed to have an oil-burning stove so that he could cook for himself for the *"enates"* (Monday, Wednesday, and Friday, the monastic fasting days, on which there is only one meal served in the evening). I, however, used it to boil my game.[10] Once I had eaten, I drank some wine and laid down to sleep. Then, when sleep had overcome me, I felt a weight on my stomach and a sense of uneasiness, as if someone had come and sat on me. I opened my

---

7   Hundreds of thousands of Greeks left for Germany (other countries as well, but primarily Germany) once the borders opened, in order to look for better opportunities.—TRANS.

8   Cf. Deuteronomy 32:15—TRANS.

9   The monk in charge of the refectory (*trapeza*).—TRANS.

10   Unless there is special dispensation, monks do not ever eat meat after their tonsure.—TRANS.

eyes and what do I see? It was the 'out-of-here'[11], the devil, with an ugly form, blood-red eyes, and two horns on his head. He looked at me and made fun of me, sticking out his tongue and laughing sarcastically. I was afraid, and tried to get rid of him by saying the Jesus prayer, but nothing happened. At last, by doing the sign of the cross, the thrice-cursed one disappeared.

"I got up in utter shock. I was shaking all over. At that moment I felt that if I died I would go straight to hell. I was lost, speechless. I did not know what I should do, or where to turn for help. Elder Athanasios, the biological brother of Elder Joseph the hesychast, saw me as I was in the midst of this shock. We had hired him as a reader, as we were short on monks. We had to pay priests to do the daily services, we paid readers, we paid workers... with everything that needed to be done to sustain the monastery those years, we could not manage otherwise. He asked:

"'What is wrong with you? Why are you so shaken up? What happened to you?'

"I explained the whole story to him, and he responded:

"'Ah, it was the wicked one who found you in a state of negligence. Out of His love, God allowed you to see what you saw so that you can start on the road to salvation.'

"'What should I do?', I asked, 'I'll do whatever you tell me, because otherwise I know I'll end up in hell.'

"'You should find a spiritual father and confess...'(I had not confessed or received communion in years), '...and after performing the penance and prayer rule that he gives you,' he continued, 'you should take Holy Communion.'

"'Where can I find a spiritual father? I do not know anyone. Please tell me, and I will go to whomever you tell me.'

"'I will give you three names, and you can decide and arrange on your own to which one you go.'

---

11 Pious Greeks prefer not to use the name of the devil at all, even as a descriptor in conversation, so to refer to him they use the phrase "ὁ ἔξω ἀπὸ δῶ", "the one who should stay away (out) of here."—TRANS.

"At that time, they did not have the habit of confessing to the abbot of the monastery.[12] They would bring in a spiritual father from outside, from the desert. He then advised:

"'At New Skete, there is Father Ephraim (later abbot of Philotheou), Father Haralambos (later abbot of Dionysiou), brothers in Christ of Elder Athanasios—that is, they, too, are disciples of Saint Joseph the Hesychast—and at Katounakia there is Father Ephraim, the well-known Katounakiote. I know all three, and I can introduce you to them. Now you choose and decide.'

"What should I do? How should I decide? I did not know! At last I decided to do the service of supplication to my protectress, the Panagia, and then write the three names on little pieces of paper and pick one: whichever name came out, I would go confess to him and do whatever he told me. I did exactly that, and the name of Father Ephraim of Katounakia came out. I was finally at peace and told myself, 'This is what God wants'. I set off for Katounakia, but after arriving I almost fell into despair. It turned out Father Ephraim was still a disciple then and not an elder, so he could not serve as an elder or spiritual father to a monk outside their brotherhood. Nevertheless, his kindness and his evident monastic love comforted me, and following his advice I went and confessed to Father Haralambos. I was very grateful and at peace, and from that moment I began trying to implement daily monastic practices in my life. I did three hundred prostrations and two hundred-knot prayer-ropes every day, and I ate whatever they had in the dining hall and nothing else, except for the allowed warm drinks.[13] I communed every fortnight, after a three-day fast from oil, and I did various tasks, aside from my normal job as *trapezaris* and chanter. The desire for ascetic life, for which I came to Athos, began to warm up again. I began saying the service of the Salutations to our Panagia every day again, which I had learned and practiced when I was a young monk but had set aside as I grew more negligent."

---

12 During the Islamic Ottoman conquest of Greece, and later during the World Wars and resulting population shifts and famine, abbots came and went, so confessing to them fell out of practice for several years.—TRANS.

13 Coffee, tea, etc.—TRANS.

Elder Arsenius began trying to live by the daily rules which Father Haralambos, his spiritual father, had given him. He began to read Saint Nikodemos, whom he found difficult to accept as a Father of the Church, Saint Symeon the New Theologian, and other ascetic books, and began to accept the strict monastic program of the new monks who came and reëstablished the former greatness of Simonopetra and to adopt it himself.

He decided to live cenobitically. He gave his second cell, which he had used as a kitchen, over to the monastery for common use, and did not hold on to any of the things he had acquired. He also began to make his warm drinks in the common kitchen of their floor, as all the other monks did.

He put his trust in Elder Emilianos, the abbot of Simonopetra, and multiplied his monastic struggles. He soaked up every one of his teachings and catechetical nourishments like a sponge. He did many prostrations, and on account of the compact nature of the structure of the cells at Simonopetra, they were heard on other floors.

This intense struggle rekindled the strong passion of his youth for the ascetic life. Now, however, he also had the suitable spiritual circumstances and the proper "trainer" for such a struggle, Elder Emilianos. They discussed the matter and he began to search for the proper place for him. He had complete trust in God and his elder and knew that he would find the place where his soul would be at peace. He first went to the cell of Saint Modestos at Karavasara but found it closed and took that as a sign that he should not live there. He then went to Ambelikia, but the lack of water and space for work were problematic, and the beautiful view of the Aegean Sea did not seem ascetic to him. He went to live at the port, but the constant thoroughfare of people coming and going did not allow for his much-desired quietness. At last he ended up in Kalamitsi; it was a small, old workhouse with only one room but with the quiet surroundings he desired.

He discussed it with his elder. They repaired it, as it had been uninhabited for many years. They made a small cistern to gather water from the stream, as there were no springs nearby, and on Bright Week he moved in. He began to live truly ascetically, hesychastically, secretly, mystically, and in the presence of God.

His program was as follows: from Monday to Saturday he was in his ascetic dwelling. He fasted, eating food without oil and in moderation. He kept vigil all night according to the practices of Saint Joseph, resting a little in the morning, then did some handiwork (he knitted prayer-ropes) and read. On Saturday afternoon, he would go to the monastery, eat with the fathers in the dining hall, participate in the Sunday service at the church, eat again in the dining hall afterwards, and then, receiving the necessary provisions for the week, walk back to his hut.

His cell was about an hour to an hour-and-a-half walk from the monastery, down near the sea. Going down to it from the monastery was easy enough, but the ascent was quite difficult, and especially when preceded by a week of asceticism, fasting, and vigils. In the summer months the creek dried up, and once he finished the water in the cistern he would only have two twenty-liter containers of water, which a certain father, who had access to a donkey, brought to his cell every Sunday.

He was always joyful, always polite, and always grateful to the elder and the fathers that took care of him. He never ceased praying, blessing, and praising. He was a true man of God: humble, ascetic, full of brotherly love, polite, deeply faithful, and with a monastic lifestyle and mindset. He was a prototype for all the younger monks. He was cheerful and silent and had something that set him aside from everyone else. In terms of physical appearance he was short, round-faced, with a small white beard, and his gold teeth showed when he smiled. He wore white socks, large woolen ones, with sandals, and a heavy white Athonite undershirt all year round.

Some of the following events show the politeness and refinement of his character, the sophistication of his conscience, and his acceptance of the will of God.

When Elder Emilianos was elected abbot of Simonopetra, Elder Arsenius was present, but due to a conscientious issue, he did not vote. When the election was done, he went and made a prostration to the new abbot saying, "I did not vote for you, but since the brotherhood elected you as abbot, I am making a prostration, and I will always be your disciple."

His gold teeth reminded him of his old, dark days of negligence. When a dental problem came up, he went to a dentist in Thessaloniki. The dentist told him that he needed some fillings, a few extractions, root canals, et cetera. Hearing that, Elder Arsenius suggested that the dentist extract all his diseased teeth and just give him dentures. After some discussion, in which the elder pressed his point strongly, the dentist agreed to do it. Once the teeth were all out, he told the dentist: "keep the gold. Do whatever you want with it. I only want the actual teeth in order to bury them in the cemetery of the monastery. It is not right to throw them out. They should be wherever the rest of my body is when I die." And that is what happened. He deeply believed in the sanctity and holiness of the whole body, and this shows how careful we must be.

When he finally moved into his cell, he had a lot of free time. He had lived in a deserted place for ten years, and he loved nature. So, in his free time and as a productive hobby, he decided to make a small garden, plant some vines, trees, et cetera. He found an old vine, left over from the old inhabitants of the hut; he took care of it, made it root, and it came back to life and developed well. He also found some wild fig-trees and wanted to graft them; Father Myron showed him how to graft, so he made grafts and grafted them. Despite the great difficulty and small percentage of success which fig grafts usually have, all of his worked. He also planted some vegetables, which also took. He was very happy about all these things; however, when it was time for prayer and his other spiritual responsibilities, his mind was constantly distracted by his garden, and his heart was being stolen away from being occupied with God to thinking about worldly things. He did not like this, so when he went to his spiritual father, Father Haralambos, and told him everything, the elder reminded him of the reason he became a monk, telling him that the devil sent this temptation, assuring that all went well with his gardening so that his mind would be stolen away from God. So, after returning to his hut, Elder Arsenius destroyed the entire garden, putting his trust in God, knowing that the Lord would take care of him. In this way he found peace and continued his *ascesis* undistracted.

His elder advised him to read the works of Abba Isaac; he did so and acquired even greater zeal in his ascetic endeavors. He did prostrations and prayed all night long. He hung some straps from the ceiling of the cell and would also use what is commonly called a "lean-on" (ἀκουμπιστήρι) so that he could remain standing all through the night. From the great number of prostrations, he got a bump on his forehead. When he took off his monastic cap it showed, and when people questioned him about it, he would say, "This head is to blame for everything. Now it is its turn." The years passed and he was very much at peace. Over time, however, his eyesight began to worsen, and he had difficulty reading. He mentioned it to his elder, who sent him to an optometrist in Thessaloniki. The doctor diagnosed it as a cataract, and told him to let it grow, and then they would operate on it. And indeed, this is what happened. However, when the time for surgery came, the doctor realized that he had made a mistake, and what he thought was a cataract was, in fact, glaucoma, which was now untreatable, as he had let it progress too far. He told Elder Arsenius that due to his misdiagnosis he would now slowly and irreversibly go blind. The elder accepted it without a single complaint, his only regret being that he would no longer be able to live in his hut. When Elder Emilianos heard, he exclaimed, "What a pity! We should have gone to another doctor for a second opinion!", to which Elder Arsenius replied, "If it would have been to the advantage of my soul, God would have enlightened you to do it. He enlightened you as He did, this is what happened, so this is what God wants from me. May His name be glorified!" He came to live at the monastery and continued the same ascetic regime, only adding daily participation in the services and frequent Holy Communion. He could not visit his spiritual father, but seeing his progress and rejoicing, Father Haralambos, despite his duties as an abbot, would come and confess him.

During Great Lent of 1981, he did the three-day fast, communed, and ate the traditional oil-free soup on Clean Wednesday. However, he then vomited and was disturbed by this. He asked his spiritual father to come and confess him, which Father Haralambos did. He comforted him, prepared him for what was to come, and left him saying, "Nothing should impede you from communing frequently."

The next week Elder Arsenius suffered a stroke, and on March 15th, 1981, during the service of Holy Unction, he handed his ascetic soul to the hands of our righteous judge, Christ.

"When the righteous dies, he leaves behind sorrow."[14] At the end of his life, Elder Arsenius struggled with all his heart, and with complete self-denial. He departed prepared for eternal life and left us an excellent example of repentance and ascesis.

May we have his blessing. Amen.

---

14   In those he has left behind (as opposed to the wicked, who leave behind joy). Proverbs 11:4. (This addition to the verse is found only in the Septuagint.)—TRANS.

Elder George of the
Cell of Saint George Phaneromenos

Father George was born in the village of Souphli in Thrace in 1902, and at his baptism was given the name Demos (surname Kozakos). When he was 23, he came to Mount Athos to become a monk, and with the Panagia's providence found a holy elder, Father Evlogius Hatzigeorgiatis[1], who took him on as a disciple. He was tonsured in 1928, taking the monastic name George in honor of Saint George, to whom the church in their cell was dedicated. There was one other member in their small cell community, Father Pachomius, the first disciple of Elder Evlogius, who had joined before Father George and later became his spiritual father. Father George found good monastic order at the cell of Saint George Phaneromenos[2] and continued the Hatzigeorgiatic tradition.

Elder Evlogius was a sanctified soul. He followed the austere ascesis of the great Hatzigeorgis and fasted from oil throughout his life. He experienced many miraculous things, and much has been written about him.

---

1   Disciple of the great Athonite ascetic George Hatzigeorgis. Hatzi is a prefix deriving from the Arabic Hajji, denoting one who had successfully completed a pilgrimage, originally to Mecca. During the Turkish occupation it came to be used by the Greek-speaking Christians throughout the former Roman empire to denote someone who had completed the pilgrimage to Jerusalem. For example, if one's name was Stephanos, after the journey it would be Hatzistephanos.—TRANS.
2   "Phaneromenos" means "revealed". That cell is dedicated to Saint George and he had done a miracle there, which is why he was given this surname.—TRANS.

When both his elders fell asleep in the Lord and he was left on his own, Father George's life was, by all appearances, the usual life of a celliot monk. The monks who knew him testified that he was good-natured and virtuous. "He would distribute produce, fresh bread, and whatever else he had amongst the other fathers. He celebrated the Divine Liturgy often, offered loukoumades[33] whenever someone visited him, and was full of joy." When cultivating his garden, he would gather up all the hazelnuts which had fallen from his hazelnut tree and clean his property. As he worked in the sweltering heat, with sweat pouring down his face, he had the Jesus Prayer, which he was trying to say unceasingly, as his aid and respite. He loved the services very much and did not leave out any parts. When he baked bread, he did so after the evening service and afterward would go out to tend the hazelnut trees. It was as if he were celebrating a vigil.

He would wake up at midnight, go to the church, and read the service for three hours, all without a heater. In his later years he read the services in his cell, as it had a fireplace. Additionally, he read the service of Supplication to the Theotokos as well as other services. From the great amount of reading, he reached points where his throat closed up and he could not utter a word.

He had appointed feastdays during which he would hold Divine Liturgy in his cell's chapel. As he was not a priest and so had to have a visiting priest officiate, he would always give a little something to the priest for his trouble.

Once, during the Akathist, while he was reading the Salutations, he saw someone inside the church. He could not make out the face and did not know whether it was Saint George or some other saint or angel. From that day on he always celebrated the Divine Liturgy on that day every year.

---

3   A Greek dessert, a round dough pastry dipped in honey, similar to a donut hole.—TRANS.

Elder George of the cell of the Revealed (Phaneromenos)

He went to the Protaton for vigils and Sunday liturgy. He had a great passion for divine worship and did not miss a single vigil. This gave him strength. He loved the church services and ecclesiastical music. Although his voice often failed him, he chanted regularly at the Protaton. In his later years, when he was a little old elder, he left his cell earlier in order to make it on time, rested at the community of the Josasaphians, and afterward continued to the vigil. On the feast of the Ascension, he would go to the vigil at the Protaton, then attend the celebration at the Iviron cell of the Ascension (commonly referred to as the cell of Davila, from the original Russian monks who built it), and after that, around noon, he would head back to his cell, which was quite a distance away, and all that in the summer heat and despite his age.

Father George was very pious and spiritually forceful; he had a great deal of simplicity,and no guile whatsoever. According to the testimony of his neighbors, "He lived a holy life." Elder Macarius the Romanian, who occasionally went and worked as a day laborer for Father George, did not have a single complaint and concurred that he was a holy man.

The grace which God gives to the worthy cannot be hidden; it reflects and pours out around them, and Father George, as all who knew him bear witness, had this grace. Once, a certain young man from outside Mount Athos was sitting at the square in Karyes observing the monks passing by. He had a votive lamp, which his grandmother had promised to donate to an Athonite monk. Out of all the fathers he saw, it was one bent-over old elder who attracted him. It was Father George, and it was to him that the young man gave the votive oil lamp.

He would tell of many miracles that happened in their cell. Saint George appeared to thieves, for which reason the cell was named Saint George Phaneromenos ('the Revealed'). There was the fish that Saint George sent for the feast, and many other things that he had seen happen to his elder Evlogius. He would recount that when his elder Evlogius prayed, an umbrella of light covered him. There were, however, some neighboring monks who did not believe his stories and mocked him, so he would not tell these things to everyone.

He himself experienced quite a few miracles and saw the providence of God, the Theotokos, and Saint George for himself. They had the icon of Saint George in their prayer corner. When someone came to them and asked to become a monk in their small community, they told him to make a prostration before the icon of the saint. At once, however, the icon fell and hit him on the head. By this they understood that the saint did not want him, and they told him to leave.

Once, while reading a service, something suddenly moved him to say the Salutations to the Virgin Mary. He left his pew and went in front of her icon, as was customary. As he was reciting the Salutations a large chunk of brick and cement fell right on the spot where he was standing a few moments earlier. Had he still been standing there, it would have killed him. But the Panagia saved him, and he immediately went to his neighbors, the Trygonades, and tearfully told them the story of the miracle.

In the year 1980, some thieves came into his cell at night. They tied him up, covered his eyes, and robbed him. They did not find any money, but they took an *epitaphios* cloth, which was woven with gold thread, gold coins dedicated to the wonderworking icon of Saint George, a censer, a gospel and a paten and chalice. As they were leaving they hit him on the face with a wet towel, telling him not to get up but to sleep tied up as he was, to which he answered with bewilderment: "What are you talking about? I want to read the service."

Later, with his face bruised from the beatings, he went and recounted everything to the Trygonades without any resentfulness or vindictiveness but only surprised as to why Saint George did not reveal the thieves. He would say: "If I wished, I would have Saint George catch them, but I felt sorry for them."

Along with these trials, he was also tempted by the devil. He would hear an inner voice, and from his great simplicity he believed it. He wanted to go to Karyes to give some of his produce to an elder, when he heard the voice say: "Don't go, he's out." He went anyway, and indeed, the elder was out. He was grateful that the voice had spoken the truth. Elder Nicholas Trygonas advised him not to believe in such things as he would fall into temptation, as indeed happened. One day, as he read the Supplication service, he heard the voice telling him that he should make the sign of the cross, and he did it. On a later night, however, he understood that all these things were temptations, and immediately he heard an angry voice by his ear cursing his beard.[4] He was terrified and ran to the Trygonades, not being able to be alone in the cell. Once he had come to himself in two to three days he returned, but he was far more careful regarding the tricks of the demons.

The long years during which Father George occupied himself with prayer brought many sweet fruits, but the simple elder did not suspect his own spiritual greatness. He confessed to the bishop Chrysostom of Rodostolos, telling him everything that happened to him, in case it was a demonic delusion. He would say, "Your eminence, the last few years strange things are happening to me. I enter my chapel, start praying," (he meant "Lord Jesus Christ, have mercy on me"), "my soul is immediately sweetened, and I do not realize how much time passes. I am pleased, of course, but the holy fathers tell us we should not trust ourselves. And since I am uneducated and my mind is not nimble enough to easily discern divine from demonic in the details of spiritual struggle, I am more afraid than others that perhaps the devil may delude me with trickery and

---

4   The beard is a symbol of a monk's dedication to God.—TRANS.

I may lose my soul. Tell me, in the name of Christ, are these things from God or from the devil?

"From the time that God took my elder to be with Him, and especially in the last few years, I've confused everything and do not know what is happening to me. When I dig in the garden and the terraces and say the Jesus prayer, I know what I am doing and can go inside when the sun is at its hottest and the heat overtakes me. But when I go into the church, it is not the same thing. I go in for Orthros when it is still pitch-black night, I venerate the icons, and then I check the votive lamps to see if any have gone out so I can light them. Then I am drawn into looking at the icon of our lord Jesus Christ with much care, and I begin the Jesus prayer. In the beginning I clearly verbalize it and understand it all. Later I lose control. I neither see the icon nor feel my lips saying anything. Everything just becomes very peaceful and it seems to me as if the Jesus prayer be inside me; I hear it and I understand perfectly in my heart, and I am pleased and very grateful. When it stops, it is already early dawn, and many times the sun is already in the sky. And so the service goes unsaid. The same thing happens when I go for vespers: night overtakes me, and I don't do vespers. The same happens when I stand in front of the icon of our Panagia. I love her very much. I like looking at her icon while saying, "Most holy Theotokos, save us," but then the same thing happens. I am afraid that the candle with which I light the votive lamps will fall from my hands while I am in this state and I will burn the church of my Saint George and myself as well; so I blow it out and put it over there before I begin the prayer."[5]

He would also say, "When I begin to read the service of preparation for Holy Communion, I feel as if there be another person inside me reading the prayers."

5   Bishop Chrysostom of Rodostolos, Γράμματα καὶ Ἄρματα στὸν Ἄθωνα, Mt. Athos 2000, p. 190-192.

When he chanted the "It is Truly Meet", tears would flow.

He advised, "In order to be save we must believe that Christ is the God-man and the Panagia is the Theotokos. And we should not leave off the Jesus prayer; a monk cannot go forward without the Jesus prayer."

In 1982 Father George was eighty years old. Forty years before, his blessed elder Evlogius had told him that he would die when he was eighty, so on the feastday of Saint George on that year, knowing that it would be his last feastday, he made special preparations to please the fathers. He asked them to chant particularly well in order to please Saint George, and he blessed them profusely.

He told everyone that he would die that year, but the doctor in Karyes did not believe it. He would say: "He's just fine, there's nothing wrong with him." And indeed, he seemed in good health. As he did every year, he gathered up his hazelnuts, his beans, and all the other produce from his garden, and on the twentieth of September he asked Elder Eugene to take him to the Trygonades brotherhood on his mule. His face had a purple hue, he was exhausted, and with tears of compunction he kept repeating, "I shall die."

He lived with the Trygonades for twenty-two days. He suffered temptations from the devil, who would not allow him to pray by bringing on dizzy spells. Before falling asleep in the Lord, he saw two silver skulls which were "dazzlingly bright." The fathers explained that those were the skulls of his elders, Evlogius and Pachomius, and they were praying that he be patient so that his skull may also become silver. He also saw a table, laden with all kinds of food and he desired to be a participant of this feast.

Sunday, October 11th, 1982 was the feastday of the Holy Fathers, towards whom he felt great reverence. At 11 o'clock that morning, God took him into His kingdom.

May we have his blessing. Amen.

Elder David of Dionysiou

Demos Floros (or, as he was later known, monk David) was born in 1889 in the village of Ktistades, in the mountains of Arta. He had two siblings. Their parents taught them piety and love for God by example, constantly instructing them to go to church and pray.

When Demos was five years old, he saw a light in the sky. His mother, to whom he showed it, did not see anything. Another time he saw the skies open, and amidst indescribable glory he saw the orders of angels and saints glorifying God, who was sitting on His throne.

From a young age he learned the skill of building and worked with a love of labor. When he was sixteen years old he was working on a certain chapel in his village. One day, as he was working, he saw a vision, which he wanted to share with his family, but when he began to speak his voice would not come out for half an hour. He then understood that he must not tell anyone what he saw, and immediately his voice returned.

Once, when he was passing by the ruins of a chapel, Saint Paraskevi appeared to him and said, "Build my church." With his holy innocence he replied, "I will build it, my lady," and venerated her. He kept his word and, being the good builder that he was, he built it.

Demos had great piety, simplicity, and purity, and because of this he could see saints, as well as the devil, from a young age.

Once, during work, his employer told him to rest and let him sleep on the bed of his own son Constantine who was away in America. Constantine, unfortunately, had become a millenarian and was influencing his family towards that heresy. As Demos went to lie down, he saw a demon on the bed, and with great strength the demon threw Demos three meters across the room.

Demos did not fear the devil. He had become accustomed to demonic temptations, as he often wrestled with demons physically. His weapons were the sign of the cross and calling upon the Virgin Mary, which made the devil disappear. One time the devil took the form of a dragon, but Demos fearlessly took him by the tail and threw him far away.

Although he loved the monastic life and wanted to become a monk since his youth, his parents stopped him. He married a young woman named Spyridoula and had two children. He continued to work and to help his family but also to struggle spiritually. Temptations were never absent.

Once, a temptation came and sat on his shoulder, but as soon as he cried out "My Panagia!" it immediately disappeared. This all happened within earshot of Spyridoula.

He would usually call the devil "thrice-cursed" and sometimes "the filthy one." He also drove him away with the exclamation of the priest, "Commemorating our most-holy, most pure, most blessed and glorious Lady, Theotokos...".

There was a time when the communists made him carry weapons from his village to another one. On the road he told them: "Christ said, 'Forgive them, for they do not know what they are doing'." They responded angrily, "Ah, so you think you can spout religion, huh? When we arrive, we'll take care of you." As soon as they arrived at the second village and set aside the weapons, he ran and hid behind a house. The communists thought that he took the road back and ran in that direction but did not find him. In this way divine Providence protected him.

Once, someone asked him for a considerable loan, and despite his own poverty, Demos agreed. That person, however, did not return what he had borrowed, and when Demos had a need of his own and reminded him of his debt, the man threatened to kill him. Then, Demos simply said to him, "May you get it from another,"[1] and

---

1   I.e. "not from me."—ED.

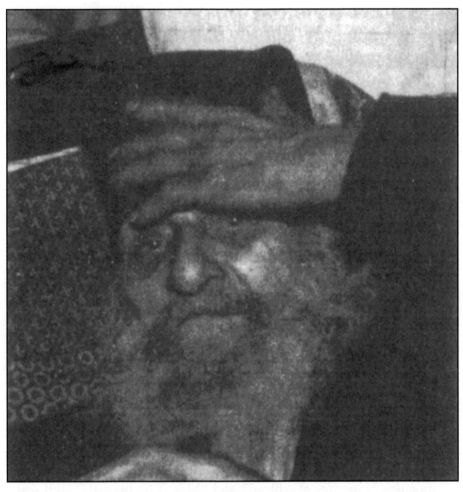

Elder David of Dionysiou

unfortunately, the saddest thing happened. That same unjust man sought a loan from someone else and, when he did not return it and instead threatened his life as well, the lender killed the dishonest man who kept borrowing money with no intention of returning it during a fight.

Once, they brought a demon-possessed woman to the monastery of the area. The whole congregation was shouting at the demon, "Get out!" Of all who were present at the time, only Demos saw the demon coming out of her mouth, in the form of a dark red rooster.

The years passed, and Demos's children grew up and had families of their own, making him a grandfather, but during all those years he never lost the burning desire to become a monk. He would say, "A divine desire was eating me up inside, the desire for Christ and for the monastic life. And so, I left my wife, my children, my relatives, my grandchildren, and my property, and came to offer my latter years to the Lord, since I could not give the earlier ones."[2]

And so, in the year 1955, at the age of sixty-six, he came to the monastery of Grigoriou. He lived there for eight months, and during that period of his novitiate he saw a vision of the two founders of the monastery.

For reasons unknown he left Grigoriou and became a monk at the neighboring monastery of Dionysiou. After the normal period of novitiate, he was tonsured a monk, taking the name David. He was enthusiastic about the monastic life and worship, of which he had been deprived for so many years, and rejoiced. He did his monastic work tirelessly and was very obedient, running like a little child to serve anywhere and everywhere he was needed. He had learned the monastic responses of "Bless"[3] and "May it be blessed,"[4] and was quiet and at peace with everyone. He did not bother or judge anyone, and sometimes he fasted more than was required. He did not dawdle in the refectory, and during his final years he would only eat what

2   Magazine Ὁ Ὅσιος Γρηγόριος, 8 (1983), p. 192.
3   I.e. "Forgive me." In Greek this is the singular aorist imperative (εὐλόγησον). The form used when asking for a priestly blessing, on the other hand, is the plural present imperative (εὐλογεῖτε).—ED.
4   This is used to show assent to a command, equivalent of "So be it."—ED.

Father Theoctistus brought to his cell. He looked as if he were dressed in rags, as he wore old and threadbare cassocks and made socks out of random pieces of fabric he found sewn together. His external appearance did not interest him, and he did not like pointless talk. He admonished his newly-tonsured fellow monk that "a little chit chat here, a little chit chat there, and the wolf gains the kid's trust and devours it," which is to say that too much idle talk harms the soul. He would never respond to those who mocked him, pretending that he did not hear them. The day that he was tonsured a great-schema monk, an older monk taunted him with scathing words, but he "became as a man that heareth not, and that hath in his mouth no reproofs" (Ps. 37:14). When that taunting monk fell asleep in the Lord, Elder David saw a vision of him in a lake, with his head just barely above water.

His cell was very unkempt and dirty and so had a lot of fleas and bedbugs. When the brotherhood of Father Haralambos came from Bourazeri, they wanted to clean it, and they threw a lot of useless rubbish into the sea. Elder David did not resist, only saying, "Glory to God that the fathers came to clean for us."

In his small, dark, humble, untidy cell he would occupy himself with the Jesus prayer. He would stay up praying at night, and in order to avoid sleep overtaking him, he would sit on a small, broken, three-legged stool when he got tired. As soon as he fell asleep, he would lose his balance, and the fall would wake him up to continue his vigil.

He had sincere humility; he was a humble coenobitic monk. As he would say, he regarded himself lower than a gnat. This humility was a shield against the many attacks of the devil, who often appeared to him.

Once, while he was praying in the chapel of the Akathist Hymn, he saw a throng of demons pass in front of him, without, however, being able to harm him.

Another time, as he was ascending the stairs of the monastery, a demon appeared to him in the form of Father Theodore, a fellow monk of the monastery, who offered him his hand to kiss. Elder David pulled back bewildered. He thought: "What is happening? Why is he giving me his hand?" And leaning down he passed under the proffered hand and went to the service.

Another time, when he was at the dependency of Monoxyliti, the devil tried to throw him off the cliff. Then Christ, the Virgin Mary, and Saint John the Baptist appeared to him, just as they were depicted in the three-paneled icon in his monastery across from the door from the refectory. The honorable Forerunner came out of the icon, took a living bodily form and saved him. He remembered this salvific event clearly for the rest of his life, and he would say, "The Lord is compassionate and merciful."

During the day at Monoxyliti he would build terraces, small huts, and produce sheds, and at night he would do a vigil from the rising of the evening star until dawn.

Other times, while he was praying, he would see a radiant young man in front of him. It was an angel. When he disappeared, he saw a host of angels glorifying God.

He told us the following: "Once, at the hour of prayer, the devil came to bother me. I immediately grabbed him and broke his head open with my fists. He got frightened and left. You see, while this was happening, I was saying the Jesus prayer."[5]

Many times he would see the demons in church, and the other fathers understood it by his reactions. He once laughed, and when they asked him why, he answered: "You didn't see the devil giving me a piece of Turkish delight so that I wouldn't sleep?"

Yet even in his cell he could not find peace from the devil, so the simple old elder fought against him in his own way: he placed a cross at every location from which the temptation entered. Afterward, the devil did not dare re-enter from that same place. For this reason, his cell came to be full of crosses; on the door, the window, the walls, even on the ceiling, there were crosses hung with string. The crosses he made were simple and self-designed. He tied two small pieces of wood with string or used strips of paper or fabric or tin in the form of a cross. They were simple, but they did the job and prevented the entrance of temptation. He would say with simplicity, "The devil presents himself to all men, but not everyone sees him. If a man has passions, wickedness, or sins, he has the devil inside his heart and

---

5   Ὅσιος Γρηγόριος, quod vide.

mind. He fears the meek and the humble but cannot do anything to them, as they are with Christ."[6]

A fellow monk in the monastery once asked him, "Brother David, do you see anything? Do you see any saints?" to which he answered, "Why do you go poking about at such things? Leave me be." Afterwards, however, after more insistent questioning, he replied with his characteristic joyful simplicity, as though relating a thoroughly natural event, "You see, yesterday I went to chant the dismissal hymn for the Archangel Michael, and he appeared in front of me in full radiance. I greeted him with a bow, and then he disappeared."

When Elder Païsius visited the monastery of Dionysiou, he also went to see Elder David in his cell. He found him wrapped up in his rags, with the curtains pulled shut so that the cell would be dark. He asked him what he was doing, and Elder David simply answered, "What do monks do?", showing his prayer-rope. When Elder Païsius asked him about his mystical spiritual experiences, he answered, "These things should not be talked about; no, they ought not to be spoken of."

The simple and uneducated elder saw many visions, starting in his childhood years, just like the prophet Ezekiel. As a monk he struggled earnestly, saying the prayer constantly and being extremely careful. He would say that the cowl protects one from scrutinizing and judging his brothers at mealtimes. He counseled monks to be obedient and have love towards each other. He considered pride the greatest of sins. He would say that whoever wants to find Christ will find Him in his own heart, even as he himself found Him, naturally, since "the kingdom of heaven is within you" (Lk 17:21).

When Elder David was ninety-four years old, he got sick for a few days in the winter. Perceiving that his end was approaching he readied himself, and on the fifth of February, 1983, he handed over his pure soul into the hands of God. Everyone forgave him and no one had a complaint against him. At his passing, a state of spiritual tranquility reigned amongst the brotherhood, and they believed that his soul found a place of rest.

May we have his blessing. Amen.

---

6   Ibid., p. 94.

Father Cyril of Karyes

Paraskevas, as he was known in the world, was from Eastern Rumelia. He was born in 1902 to Stavros and Melpomeni Kotso-mopoulos in the village of Pyrgos, which now belongs to Bulgaria.[1] His family moved to Greece, and when Paraskevas came of age, he found work in a bank.

One day a venerable Athonite elder, Father Eugene from the cell of the Holy Trinity above Karyes,[2] came to the bank. Paraskevas was so impressed when he saw him that he immediately ran to assist him. When the business was completed, he implored the elder to wait two or three days to allow him to settle his affairs and then to let him come back to the Holy Mountain with him. Indeed, that same day Paraskevas submitted his resignation, settled his affairs, bid farewell to his relatives, and followed Father Eugene, who would later become his elder, to Mount Athos. He arrived in 1920, at the age of eighteen. Father Eugene's brotherhood was good, keeping a monastic typicon, reading all the services in the church, and not leaving anything out. During the Hours they would ring a small bell, which would signal for the brothers to leave their work, gather in the church, and read the service. They occupied themselves with

---

1   Eastern Rumelia (modern-day southeastern Bulgaria), as well as Northern Epirus (modern-day southern Albania) and much of Asia Minor, were historically Greek, in both ethnicity and language. After the Ottoman conquests and through the world wars there was a shift of borders, and many Greeks were displaced or found themselves living in a different country.—TRANS.

2   This cell, nicknamed Profourni ("before the bakery") probably due to its location on the road, belonged to the monastery of the Great Lavra.—TRANS.

Father Cyril of Karyes

farm work, chiefly olive and hazelnut production and vegetable gardening, but they also made monastic head coverings, for which reason they were called 'kalymmavchades.'[3]

Paraskevas gave himself over to monastic struggles with exceedingly great zeal and perfect obedience. For this reason he was tonsured the very next year and given the name Cyril. It seems that even before his monastic life, while still in the world, he was engaged in spiritual struggles and was very pious. Elder Eugene's soul was at rest with his new disciple, and his neighbors, as many as are still alive, consider him to have been a delightful monk. They spoke with wonder regarding his life, noting that "he prayed all night and only slept for two hours. He fasted a great deal and was polite and kind to everyone. No one ever saw him get angry when he was insulted or slandered. He was very humble, and when misunderstandings occurred, he was the first to do a prostration and say, 'Forgive me.'"

There was a time when he overheard some woodworkers, hired by the monks for a job, blaspheming the divine. When he heard this, he immediately went to them, fell at their feet, and wept. When they saw his reaction they were greatly shocked. They sought his forgiveness, promising that they would never blaspheme again.

Other times, when hired workers from outside Athos would share inappropriate jokes, he would humbly ask them to pray and not speak such filthy words, after which he would leave, discerning it to be the best thing. He did not quarrel with them but tried to arouse their sensitivity and love of righteousness.

During the day he would wear himself out in the arduous chores of the cell, and at night he would light a gas lamp and study. Sleep would overtake him on account of his fatigue, and his nose was almost always burnt, because as soon as sleep overtook him he would lean forward and onto the lamp, get burnt, and immediately wake up. He had a great thirst for learning and read many patristic books. He gave the impression that he was learned, and whatever questions were asked of him always received appropriate answers.

---

3   The kalymmavchi (Greek καλυμμαύχιον) is one of the pieces of clerical headwear worn by Orthodox Christian monks and clergy. In appearance it is similar to a stovepipe hat without a brim.—TRANS.

His purity, virtue, and piety made his elder decide to ordain him a deacon on the 4th of January, 1953, and the very next day, against his will, at the age of 51, he was ordained a priest.

As a priest, he was guileless, pure, and most pious. He celebrated the Divine Liturgy with care and piety and recited the Gospel beautifully and with feeling. He also served in the Protaton and was the first priest in the procession of the icon of the "It Is Truly Meet" (*Axion Estin*). He always willingly went to serve at the feasts of the patron saints of the neighboring cells[4] and was always serious. Excess words never escaped his mouth and he never judged anyone. He inspired respect and on account of his virtues shone like a morning star.

For all these reasons, they wanted to make him a spiritual father, but he declined, saying, "I have seen seven spiritual fathers that did not decompose."[5]

Until his old age Father Cyril would force himself[6] to fast, pray, and keep the nightly vigil. His disciple, Father Paul, would chide him for keeping vigil at his advanced age, and on account of humility, Father Cyril would not say anything, preferring to struggle secretly so as not to irritate Father Paul and cause him to yell.

He fell asleep in the Lord on June 12th, 1985 at the age of 82. He was admired by all the fathers who knew him, and all of them said that he was very virtuous, one of the unrepeatable monks who came through the area of Karyes in these last years.

May we have his blessing. Amen.

---

4   Many monastic cells have no ordained priests amongst the number of their brotherhood, and so they have to ask neighboring priests to come and celebrate Divine Liturgy. —TRANS.

5   After a certain period, usually three years, monks' remains are exhumed and their bones are taken to the ossuary. If their bodies have not yet dissolved, it is seen as either incorruptibility due to great holiness or the opposite, a demonic, unnatural lack of decomposition, a sign of grave sin. In this case it refers to the latter.—TRANS.

6   Or "exercise violence on himself;" see Mt. 11:12.—ED.

The hesychast Phanurius of Kapsala

Hesychast Phanurius of Kapsala

Elder Phanurius was born on July 12th, 1898, in Tecostl, Romania. His parents were named Stephen (Mandras) and Helen, and at his baptism he was given the name Basil. He was the firstborn of a large family of fourteen children, and his parents were very pious. Even though they loved him exceedingly, they believed that the first child belonged to God, according to scripture, "Every male that openeth the womb shall be called holy to the Lord,"[1] so when he was fifteen years old they sent him to Mount Athos, to the Skete of the Forerunner, where his uncle was a monk and the secretary of the skete. He came to the Holy Mountain in 1913, and in 1915 became a monk with the name Phanurius.

He lived there for thirty years, struggling with zeal and great piety, but he longed to live a hesychastic life, so he came to the cell of Saint Theophilus in Kapsala which was dedicated to Saint Basil. Saint Theophilus the Myrrhstreamer had also lived in that cell, and his holy relics were buried under the altar. Sts. Gerasimus of Kefalonia and Nikodemos the Athonite had also lived there, so it was a very holy cell and a place of veneration in Kapsala. Whoever visited the cell of Elder Phanurius for the first time would ask if anyone was living there, as he had perfect passionless detachment and all his effort was toward spiritual things, and so his cell looked uninhabited.

He fasted until the ninth hour every day,[2] and his mouth was often dry from fasting and thirst. He fasted so assiduously that his body became unaccustomed to food with oil and could not tolerate it. He

1   Luke 2:23.—TRANS
2   3pm, the ninth hour after dawn.—TRANS

lit many vigil lamps, both in front of the icons in his cell and in the church. He did constant vigils with the prayer-rope and always read from the Psalter and the New and Old Testaments. He also read and loved the writings of Abba Isaac. He was an excellent chanter and knew Byzantine music well.

In his little cell he felt as though he were in paradise. When he was younger, he would go to other cells to work and earn money for food. At some point, however, he saw the saints of his cell in a vision, and they said to him: "Do not go work in other cells. We will take care of you." From then on he never lacked anything. He neither sold handiwork nor took the pension to which he was entitled. He did not even go to Karyes to buy things. The Panagia and the saints of his cell provided everything for him.

Elder Phanurius had a true sense of monasticism. Someone gave him a fancy overcoat for the cold, but he did not wear it, even though he needed it; he gave it to someone else. Another neighboring monk brought him water with a hose, and offered to install a tap so that he could have running water as well, but he did not accept. He preferred to go and draw water with a pitcher from the site of Saint Theophilus, further away, until he got old and could no longer carry water on his own. He loved silence and tradition. When someone told him that they were building a road into Kapsala, he was saddened, saying, "Can you believe it? A road in Kapsala!"[3]

Elder Phanurius was very pious, ascetic, and spiritually sober. His daily schedule was as follows: after doing Vespers on the prayer-rope and eating a small, oil-free meal with some bread rusk, he rested for about an hour. Afterwards he began the service with the prayer-rope until tears flowed. Thereafter, he wept while praying for all the world, which his love-filled heart embraced.

Elder Phanurius had the spiritual gifts of tears, unceasing remembrance of death, and noetic prayer. He would say: "I think about where God will place me when I die, since I am a sinful man," and his tears would run without stopping. "I am always crying," he said. "Sins are not cleansed without tears. A man must have fear and love

---

3   Kapsala had previously been inaccessible by car, and he feared the loss of stillness and silence that a road would bring.—TRANS

for God. These two are related. You should ask God for them, and He will grant them." When they asked for his counsel, he would tell them to do whatever the books (the Gospels) said.

Elder Phanurius was captivated by love for Christ. Once, a certain monk visited him and knocked on the door saying the traditional monastic greeting of "through the prayers of our Holy Fathers…". The elder was outside sitting under a tree, reading, but he went and opened the door, bowed to the monk, and they spoke. Afterwards when the monk left, the elder left the door open so that no one would have to knock, and ran back to his book.

Other times he would sit and read outside in his yard, in a corner that was not visible from the outside, leaving the cell door open so that pilgrims could go in and venerate. Whoever knew his practice would go in and venerate without interrupting his study and prayer. If they were not aware, he would lead them to the church and speak to them about Saint Theophilus, usually with tears in his eyes.

Other times he was so occupied with intense spiritual labor and divine contemplation that when someone knocked, he opened the door without looking at the visitor's face, and silently led them to the church while internally continuing the Jesus prayer.

A certain young monk visited Elder Phanurius and asked him for some spiritual advice to benefit and correct the passions in his soul, to which the elder answered, "My child, now that you are young you must struggle to make a good start in spiritual practices, because you will end your monastic life the way you began it."

He was a great ascetic. He would humbly say, "Since I am lazy and have difficulty waking up in the morning, I start the service the evening before and don't sleep at night." He stood so much and for so long that he suffered a hernia. Fathers Xenophon and Herodion the Romanians testified with amazement to his asceticism and to the violence which he imposed on himself.

Father Xenophon would say that not even the ascetics of old reached Elder Phanurius' level of ascesis. He would pray day and night non-stop for many days. He had incredible stamina. He would come all the way from Daphne carrying his large satchel without stopping to rest, even though he was small in frame.

When his neighbor, Elder Michael the Romanian, got sick, Elder Phanurius, despite his own advanced age, went every day to help him with his needs.

Through such supernatural struggles, he came to have equally supernatural spiritual experiences and divine visions. He saw Sts. Theophilus and Basil, who corrected him, as he had been negligent in something. Elder Phanurius would say that Saint Theophilus had also appeared to his predecessor, who kept rabbits and owned a shotgun, and told him to leave (since he would not be corrected), saying that this was a hermitage. Someone else went to destroy a wall in order to take the relics of Saint Theophilus which were buried inside, but flames shot out. Other times, myrrh flowed on the wall from the relics of Saint Theophilus. In such a sanctified environment, Elder Phanurius lived a holy life. He would say, "When an angel comes here, the whole night is very peaceful; when a demon comes, the whole place stinks."

Once he saw the three hierarchs and asked Saint Basil the Great, for whom he had an especially great reverence since he had received his name at baptism, which had prompted him to live in a cell dedicated to him: "Tell me, please, do I still owe a lot?" To which the saint answered, "You're alright."

Another time he saw Saints Basil and Theophilus, and they told him to try harder in his spiritual life.

He had an excellent memory until the very end. He kindly received whatever pilgrims arrived at his cell and took care of them. After they venerated, he would briefly answer their queries with soul-benefiting counsel. His remarkable memory permanently recorded all the pilgrims, for whom he prayed to God on his prayer-rope.

Three times, from piety and zeal, he went to Jerusalem as a pilgrim.

He was not a zealot, but he was in great anguish of heart over the situation that existed in the church with the schisms and heresies. He was gullible, since "the simple believeth every word" (Prov. 14:15).

One time he visited a neighbor and found him listening to the radio. Elder Phanurius prophetically told him to throw the radio away because otherwise it would lead him to marriage. The neighbor did not listen to him, and unfortunately Elder Phanurius' prophesy came to pass.

Starting in 1984, he began to prepare for his earthly departure. He sent his few possessions to the Romanian Skete of the Honorable Forerunner, which was his place of repentance, and then went to all his neighbors and asked for forgiveness.

He enclosed himself in his beloved silence and intensified his prayer and tears. In 1986 he saw Sts. Theophilus and Basil and they told him, "You will not celebrate New Year's here. You will come and we will celebrate together." He told someone and that person told him not to believe in dreams.

"But this was not a dream!" he answered.

Two fellow monks had visited him, and while leaving said, "We'll come back later, Elder," to which he replied, "You won't find me. I'll be dead." He specifically told another monk that he would fall asleep in the Lord before the first of the year.

On December 18, the eve of the first of the year (with the new calendar of 1986), his neighbors found him asleep in the Lord. On the day of his funeral there was much snow and only three fathers attended. His tomb was full of water and the relics of Father Phanurius were light as a feather, so they floated in the water. When they exhumed his relics to move his bones to the ossuary, they found that a bone in his foot had been broken and healed incorrectly. Who knows what martyric pains Elder Phanurius suffered, without ever revealing them, even to a doctor!

May we have his blessing. Amen.

Abbot Andrew of Saint Paul's

Abbot Andrew of Saint Paul's

Abbot Andrew of Saint Paul's was born in the village of Angona, in the island of Kefalonia, on January 22, 1904. His parents, Gregory Evangelatos and Vasiliki Panagoulatou, named him Angelos at his baptism. They did not stay in the village where he was born for long but moved further north.

Angelos was pious and his life was one of care. He had a desire to be a monk and dedicate his life to God. As a layman he knew the Salutations to the Virgin Mary by heart and prayed them every day. He could not sleep, no matter how much work he might have done during the day, without saying the Salutations. When he grew up he became a policeman. He loved both the church and prayer, and when at last he decided to become a monk, he did it.

Even though Kefalonia had monasteries, he preferred to become a monk further away. He went into voluntary exile so that no one would know him and his relatives would not bother him. He heard that there was a large monastery dedicated to Saint Luke in Livadeia. He decided to go there. He did not know exactly where it was, but he was determined to leave for Livadeia on Monday. The previous day, Sunday, he went to church in Lixouri. He went early, and as soon as he entered the church he saw a tall, young, athletic man in ancient military garb with a short toga. He was not curious about him, and when the young man gestured for him to come closer, he did not pay attention. The young man went behind the altar and gestured again, and again Angelos did not pay attention and did not go into the altar. He sat in his seat, and when the liturgy ended he went home.

On Monday he began his journey for Livadeia. He first went to Patra and from there to Athens. In Patra he met a monk, greeted him, and confided his mission to him, telling him that he was going to become a monk at Saint Luke's monastery in Livadeia. The monk replied, "What will you do there? Come to the Holy Mountain, to the Garden of the Virgin Mary; there is only one Mount Athos." The monk told him a number of things that made Angelos change his mind and decide to go with him to the Holy Mountain. They arrived in Piraeus, went to Thessaloniki by boat, and from there to Daphne. The monk was from Esphigmenou, but Angelos went to venerate at Simonopetra. Once there, he asked if there was another monastery close by, and then went to venerate at Grigoriou, Dionysiou, and then Saint Paul's by foot, all on the same day. It was September of 1934, and he arrived at Saint Paul's during Vespers. He went into the church to venerate and saw an icon of Saint George on the right side of the iconostasis. He looked carefully, looked again, and wondered, "Where have I seen this icon before?" Then he remembered. "I haven't seen the icon. I saw the man (Saint George). He was the one in the church of the Pantokrator in Lixouri! It was he! I will not leave. I will stay here." And so he stayed, making a prostration and asking to become a novice.

At that time, the abbot was Elder Seraphim. Seeing his maturity, his piety, his willing obedience, and his ascetic zeal, he tonsured him a monk after only four months, on January 16, 1935, and on the twenty-fifth of the same month they found him worthy to receive the Great and Angelic Schema with the name Andrew. One month later they ordained him a deacon, and six months after that, on July 28, a priest. This all took place in the span of only ten months, and now, at age of thirty-one, he was Hieromonk Andrew. Then he understood why Saint George was signaling for him to come. He was calling him first to his monastery and then to the Holy Altar (meaning the priesthood). Everything had been foretold.

While he was struggling and working through the various monastic jobs, Father Andrew felt drawn to hesychasm. At that time, Father Gerasimus Menagias, who hailed from Kefalonia, was living ascetically in the desert of Saint Basil, and would occasionally visit Saint Paul's.

Father Andrew got to know Father Gerasimus and desired to live with him. He pleaded with Abbot Seraphim at length, and at last the abbot gave him a blessing. In 1938 he went to Saint Basil's and lived with Father Gerasimus for two and a half years. During that time he met other ascetics, as well as Elder Joseph the Hesychast, for whom he had a great reverence. He considered him a saint and defended him when he would hear others criticizing him.

He considered it his great fortune to have also met Father Sophrony the Russian, with whom he was spiritually joined. He understood the spiritual wealth and divine grace that the then deacon Sophrony had; he had great reverence for him, and sought to keep in touch with him.

One day in 1939, Father Andrew and deacon Sophrony had gone outside to gather snails. Suddenly they saw the shadow of a man at a distance and observed that he was nearly naked. They understood that it was one of the naked ascetics and they ran to catch him. Once he noticed them, however, the ascetic ran to hide. Deacon Sophrony got tired and Father Andrew, who was younger, asked him:

"Should I run to catch up to him?"

"If you can, then run."

Father Andrew took off running, and when he got to within two meters of the ascetic, he shouted:

"Stop, man! I only want your blessing. If you are not a demon, bless me."

He got near him and grabbed him by the hand.

"If you love God, let me be," the ascetic told him.

"It is because I love God that I ran to catch up to you."

He saw that the ascetic was wearing a shabby hair sack around his waist, and nothing else, not even shoes or socks. As it was March, and so still very cold, he said to him:

"How can you be like this? Can I bring you clothes?"

"I don't want them."

"Do you want any bread or anything else?"

"No."

"Can I bring you something? Just as a blessing to me."

"Bring me a little salt."

Abbot Andrew of Saint Paul's as a young monk

"Where should I bring it?"

"Leave it on that rock."

The next day they brought the salt, left it on the rock, and lay in wait. The salt remained there, and the ascetic did not appear again.

Father Andrew also told the following story: "Father Gerasimus was a personal friend of Saint Nectarius, who had given him a photograph of himself and a prayer-rope. At that time, some people at Saint Basil's doubted the holiness of Saint Nectarius. Father Gerasimus, in order to prove that the holy bishop of Pentapolis was indeed a saint, took a basin, put flour and water in it, mixed them, and put the prayer-rope that he had received from Saint Nectarius on top. Then, without yeast, the mixture began to rise on its own.

"I do not want any other proof," Father Andrew would say.

Father Andrew met many great ascetics during his time at Saint Basil's and benefited by their example. He struggled fervently and, as he was in touch with his monastery during that time, after two and half years he decided to return to the place of his repentance. He then told Abbot Seraphim, "I met many saints in the desert, and also a holy deacon. If we manage to bring him here as a spiritual father, he will help us greatly." Abbot Seraphim agreed. "Of course, since you think so, we will do it," so they went and pleaded with deacon Sophrony to come. He wanted silence but considered that this offer may be from divine providence, as Saint Silouan had told him, "When anyone asks for your help, do not deny it. As a spiritual father you should be discerning and not excessive." So, he considered that the time had come for the saint's words to be realized. On the feast of the Presentation of the Lord in 1941 they ordained him a priest. He lived at Karoulia for one more year, and after that he moved to the cell of the Holy Trinity. The monastery gave him koumbania,[1] and he gave them icons he painted and confessed the fathers. He helped a great deal and he saved the monastery from many dangers during those difficult years of the German occupation. And all this thanks to the foresight of Father Andrew.

---

1   Cretan *loukoumades*. —TRANS

After Father Andrew returned from the desert, he became the monastery's officiating priest for twenty years. During the break in services before the Divine Liturgy he slept not in a bed but sitting in a chair, so that no temptation would come to him. He celebrated the Divine Liturgy every day, and afterwards he would go down to Saint Tryphon in the Little Orchards and plow the fields with the wooden plow and oxen. Another, older priest celebrated Vespers. Father Andrew would plow all day or go to the mountain with the woodcutter fathers. He returned late, just before dusk, and in the morning he would again do the services and Divine Liturgy. He sacrificed his life for the monastery and all the fathers loved him for it; therefore later, when there was a need, they elected him abbot twice.

Since the day he left to be a monk, Father Andrew did not send a single word to his relatives to inform them where he was. They all thought he had died, except his mother who, through intuition, would say, "My child has not perished. He is in a good place." After some years a boat docked at the port, and someone from his village happened to be on board. He recognized Father Andrew and spoke with him, but the monk told him not to tell anyone, even if they were looking for him. The man, however, informed his relatives, and his mother sent him a joyful letter. She wrote that she wanted to see him, as she was not going to live for much longer. He then responded to her letter, asking: "Do you want to see me in this life or the next? Because it cannot be both. Choose." She wrote back, "In the next, my child," and so died without seeing him.

After his mother had passed away, his father came to see him in order to be comforted. He was a little old man and only intended to come for a few days and afterwards go back home and do the forty-day memorial for his wife. The days passed, and Father Andrew asked him:

"Aren't you going to leave?"

"No, I will stay here. I like it."

He still had a daughter and many reasons to return to the world, but he was pious and had a cultivated soul. When abbot Seraphim learned of his decision to stay, he asked him:

"Do you want me to make you a monk?"

"If you will give me this gift, may God grant you many years."

And so, at the age of eighty-eight, they tonsured him a monk, giving him the name Symeon. Despite his age, he was the first person in church for the services. He was hard of hearing, so during the readings he would go and sit next to the readers' stand in order to hear every word. He was also first in line for Holy Communion, and Abbot Seraphim would say, "You see this stump? He is going to surpass us all."

In 1960 abbot Seraphim fell asleep in the Lord and Father Andrew became the abbot. The next year, Father Symeon, who was ninety-six, got sick and they brought him to the geriatric ward. Father Andrew noted: "I do not think you're well. Shall we commune you? To which the old monk replied, "Let's do as you see best." Father Andrew brought the Host, and after Father Symeon, with considerable difficulty, managed to say the 'Our Father' he received Holy Communion. His son then asked:

"How do you feel?"

"As if I were going to a wedding."

Father Andrew took the Holy Chalice back to the church and then returned to the geriatric ward, but Father Symeon had already fallen asleep in the Lord.

One time, Father Andrew went to visit Elder Anthimus at the monastery hospital. The elder did not have long to live. Father Andrew asked him: "Do you want us to bring you anything? A spiritual father? A doctor?" The elder did not understand; he just leaned against the bed's iron railing and began to say the service of the Salutations noetically. Every time he came to 'Rejoice, O Bride unwedded,' the little old elder would make the sign of the cross. As soon as he finished the service, Elder Anthimus made the sign of the cross three times and fell asleep peacefully.

When Elder Gregory was in his last days, he did not speak. He had lost his senses, and the brothers called Father Andrew to commune him. He gave him Holy Communion, but Elder Gregory could not swallow it. Father Andrew then told the brothers to prepare some tea, and slowly, with a small spoon, a bit at a time, he fed him the tea until he was able to swallow. At that point, Elder Gregory spoke and said, "Thank you very much. May God reward you."

Father Andrew would say the following about the fathers who fell asleep in the Lord during his time at the monastery: "There are two or three whose fate I'm not sure of, but all the rest whom I saw went to the Kingdom of Heaven."

Two and a half years after he was elected abbot, Father Andrew resigned over a disagreement about an administrative matter, saying, "Why did I go and get mixed up in all this?"

Father Eusebius then took over as abbot. He was pious, virtuous, and ascetic, but he would not make any concessions for anyone. After six years he resigned, and in July of 1969 the fathers elected Father Andrew again. He exercised *economia* when it came to others but remained severe and exacting on his own conscience. He was strict on himself, but exhausted every form of sensitivity and consideration for the other fathers.

Abbot Andrew was a classic, practical Athonite. He counseled the fathers not to leave aside their prayer rule and to make a complete and thorough confession. He was in favor of frequent communion, saying, "If a coenobitic monk is obedient, loves the services, confesses honestly, and doesn't judge anyone, he is ready for paradise." He abolished the three-day oil-free fast before Holy Communion and offered Holy Communion every Thursday and Saturday.

He was the first abbot at Saint Paul's who agreed to hear monks' confessions. Every day between 1:30 and 3:00pm he received them in the abbot's quarters. He listened to confessions quietly. If someone told him, "Elder, I failed in this or that", he would answer: "What can we do? We must look to the mercy of God." But if someone told him that he judged others, then he became very strict and said sharply, "When did you become God? Are you not ashamed of yourself?" and afterwards led the monk towards repentance with peaceful words. He completely trusted Father Dionysius from Little Saint Anne's and went to him for confession, even though Father Dionysius was much younger than he was.

His love for the fathers was boundless, and he did not treat the good monks differently from the bad. He was merciful, and though those years were difficult and material goods were sparse, he gave generously. Someone once asked him for a pair of socks and he gave him two. When someone asked him for a pair of pants, he gave him two as well, telling him: "You can wear the one while you wash the other." He ordered the monk responsible for the refectory to give alms freely to both known fathers and strangers, saying, "When they need something, where will they find it? Will they ask their relatives, or run hither and thither?"

He was polite and always tried to honor and help others. When someone wanted something, before they even had to ask, he would say, "Do you need anything, my dearest one?" He usually referred to others as "my child," and this expressed his entire internal disposition towards his monks. He had great love and consideration for the fathers. When appropriate, however, he became strict, but this strictness stemmed from his love and desire to help the fathers. If he heard gossip or excessive idle talk in the kitchen, he would come and tell them to stop. He would not believe in visions of light or angels if he could not thoroughly verify them.

He would say the following about the remembrance of God: "Saint Mary of Egypt saw the icon of the Virgin Mary once, when it stopped her from entering the church, and this memory strengthened her for forty years alone in the desert. We want to see this thing and that, and we still lack the remembrance of God."

In the year 1970, during lent, he suffered a gastric hemorrhage. Father Democletus, the doctor, told him that his condition was very serious, and he had to go out into the world, as this illness had to be treated scientifically. The abbot replied: "The Panagia is our science. I am not leaving the Holy Mountain." He had been a monk for thirty-six years, and in all that time had never left Mount Athos. The doctor then said: "We should obey you every day of our life, and you should obey us now. If we do not take you to the doctor, you will die." The abbot then acquiesced. "On account of obedience, I am in your hands. I'll do whatever you think best."

They took him to Thessaloniki; he was operated on and returned healthy.

In October of 1974, Abbot Andrew resigned from his position and went to live hesychastically in a dependency of the monastery on the Holy Mountain at Monoxyliti, where there was a church dedicated to Saint Nicholas, for whom he had great reverence.

It was there in 1975 that some zealot monks from Esphigmenou visited him. Their abbot had passed away, and as they were afraid that they might be exiled from the monastery, they were begging him to take on the abbacy himself. His humanity was touched by the things he heard and the zealots' entreaties, but he could not decide. He was afraid that, while on the one hand it would be a shame if he did not help Esphigmenou, on the other hand, how could he leave the place of his repentance at such an advanced age? He prayed to the Panagia and Saint Nicholas to enlighten him, and one day he saw a little old priest coming up from the sea path below. When he arrived, he greeted him, asked for the road to Karyes, and was shown it. The former abbot, however, asked him for his name and where he was from, to which the old priest answered that he was from Cyprus and his name was Nicholas. Father Andrew was not a curious man and would never normally ask questions, but by divine inspiration he did it. The little old man continued on his way to Karyes, but as soon as Father Andrew went inside, he thought, "Ah, it's lunchtime and I didn't invite the poor man to come and eat. Where will he go, hungry as he must be?"

He went back outside and called for him, but did not see him. The road for Karyes was visible for at least half a mile, so he should have been able to see him, yet he was nowhere to be seen. He started down the road calling out for the priest. Nothing. He thought, "it's a pity I didn't manage to get to him in time," then went inside, not giving it any more thought, sat, ate, and then slept. A little while later he woke up filled with joy and decided that "I belong at Saint Paul's, not at Esphigmenou, and not in the abbacy. I am no good for a second or third run at being abbot." He went into the church, looked at the icon of Saint Nicholas and realized with surprise that the saint in the icon was the same as that priest that passed by earlier and disappeared. He then thought, "But why didn't my mind clear earlier?" He mentioned the event to Father Dionysius, his spiritual father, who told him: "It was Saint Nicholas. He came and took away the weight that you had on your soul."

A little while afterward, during his hesychastic residence at Monoxyliti, there was a terrible storm. The day after, he thought to go down to the sea to gather up any driftwood that the sea had brought out but also in case someone needed his help.

While he was collecting the wood which had washed up from the sea, he saw a human shadow sitting on a rock. He immediately thought that it may be some passerby or a shipwrecked survivor, so he ran to help. When he drew near, he was surprised to see a nun sitting on the rock holding an open book and pen. Shocked and perplexed, he asked her:

"What are you doing here, ma'am? Do you need any help?"

"No, I do not want help," answered the apparent nun. "I am the Lady of this place and I do this job from the one end of Mount Athos to the other."

"And what are these books you're holding?"

"The books are the entrances, departures, and residence records of the Athonite fathers. But this book you see here contains the names of those who stay and complete their life on the Holy Mountain, and these names are written in the Book of Life."

After the conversation, as the apparent nun did not want help, Father Andrew went back up to the dependency. That afternoon he went to the church to read Vespers, and when he saw the icon of the Theotokos on the iconostasis, something happened inside him and he began to feel joy and ebullience thinking of the nun with the books. He also saw the icon's vigil-lamp swaying on its own and quickly went back down to the seaside, hoping that he would make it to the nun in time, his mind now clear and certain that it was the Panagia. But he did not find her as he had hoped, and sadness descended on his soul, as he thought that because of his sins he was not worthy to see her again. Then, drawing near the rock where she had sat, he sensed a sweet and heavenly smell which flooded the whole place. In this way the Theotokos verified her presence and informed him that it was indeed she with whom he had spoken face to face.

He then invited Father Dionysius to Monoxyliti, explained the incredible sight, and the spiritual father verified that it was, indeed, the Panagia. The elder then asked Father Dionysius not to tell anyone, "as they'll think me a saint, and then all sorts of people will be coming and going."

Father Andrew's piety towards the Virgin Mary was rewarded by his ability to see her and speak to her while still alive. He was a great spiritual warrior. He worked hard at Monoxyliti, and wore himself out despite his age, but he never neglected the church services and his prayer rule. If, once in a while, he did not read the Psalter during the service, he read it in his cell. He also had a problem with his stomach, and when it hurt he sat down, but he always read the Psalter.

Elder David said, "Once I was plowing at Monoxyliti and an ox got sick. I called Father Andrew, he read a prayer, and the ox immediately got up."

When Father Andrew resigned, Parthenius was elected abbot. Father Andrew supported him greatly, and would say, "My dearest ones, we have an abbot full of the grace of the Holy Spirit."

When he was a little old man and stayed in his cell, as he was no longer able to go down to the services, the abbot went to see him and ask if he needed anything. "Listen, my child: I do not need anything. I have everything, and I lack nothing. Another reason I cannot ask for anything is because I am afraid Christ may damn me for my ingratitude in asking for things I don't need, but thank you very much!"

Father Andrew told the following story: there was a certain lay worker at the monastery, a very virtuous man. He became extremely ill, and as he (Father Andrew) was both resident priest and monastery bursar, he offered to him to tonsure him a monk. The layman joyfully accepted, the tonsure went ahead, and the man fell asleep on the feastday of the Presentation of the Lord, which was the feast of the monastery. Father Andrew would often say, "This worker must have been very virtuous indeed for the Panagia to take him on the feastday of the Presentation."

Yet he, also being virtuous, was counted worthy to fall asleep in the Lord during the vigil of the very same feastday.

In 1987, on the night before the feastday of the Presentation of the Lord, the feast of the monastery, a monk brought food to Father Andrew. He ate, crossed his hands, and passed away in his seat. After the vigil they performed his funeral and informed his friend and fellow ascetic, Elder Sophrony of Essex, that he had fallen asleep, to which he replied, "I know, I was there."

At his funeral, whoever kissed his hand felt that he was kissing the hand of a saint, as if it were a holy relic. During the funeral service, his spiritual father, Father Dionysius of Little Saint Anne's, recounted the story of the appearance of the Panagia at Monoxyliti in detail. The fathers had not known before then.

On August 3, 1994, during the transfer of his relics, his right hand gave off a sweet scent, as if it were holding incense. Father Sophrony of Saint Paul's perceived it, as well as other fathers. It seems that God gave him this grace for his generous almsgiving during his life.

May we have his blessing. Amen.

Elder Evdokimus of Saint Paul's

Elder Evdokimus of Saint Paul's

Elder Evdokimus of Saint Paul's Monastery was born Evangelos Traulos in the year 1910, in the village of Phanari in Karditsa. When he was discharged from the army, he told them to put down "Daphne" as his forwarding address. Indeed, he did not return to his village, but came straight to Mount Athos to become a monk. He was headed to a different monastery, but he stopped over at Saint Paul's for one night, liked the monastic order there, and stayed. He was educated by the standards of the time, having graduated middle school, so they accepted him and the abbot had him as an assistant. He was tonsured in 1935.

His mother, sisters, and brother did not want him to become a monk, and once he was tonsured, he never went back to his village to see his relatives. He only left the Holy Mountain after thirty years, and then only because he had an unceasing nosebleed and the doctor was afraid he might die.

One year there was a great earthquake, and the fathers slept outside in the back garden on the terraces due to the aftershocks. Elder Evdokimus did not go with them but slept in his cell as usual. When they asked him why he was not afraid, he answered: "I came here to be at this monastery. If the Panagia wants to destroy the monastery, why would I want to live?" He lit the vigil-lamps and did not leave the monastery at all during the entire duration of the earthquake.

He did not do many prostrations or fasts. He occupied himself with the Jesus prayer. He never lay down. His cell was filled with useless things. He never closed the window, whether it was winter or summer. The only empty space in his cell was a path from the door to the bed.

He slept sitting up, covered with a blanket. They asked him why he did not light a fire for warmth, and he would answer, "Where are the icicles? I do not see any icicles to need a fire for warmth." He would answer the same thing when they told him to close the window.

He was naturally funny and he never judged. You could curse him with the foulest language, he would stand silent for a while, and then say, "Alright, father, thank you," and leave.

He was loved by all and had no guile. He was always willing and obedient to any that asked him to perform some task. You could execrate him, and then call his name, "Father Evdokimus!" and he would respond "Bless"[1] with good humor and willingness, as though nothing had happened.

Once, when some monks were discussing some matter pertaining to the monastery, Elder Evdokimus voiced his opinion. Another monk, succumbing to demonic temptation, shouted at him, saying: "You be quiet! You are not the abbot!" The elder bowed his head and said, "Forgive me, you are right."

In the winter after the prescribed meal, he would go directly to the church, sit in a stall [*stasidi*], pull down his cowl so that his face could not be seen, take out his prayer-rope and say the Jesus prayer. A monk once asked him what he was doing, to which he answered, "I'm fighting him (the devil). See my cannon?" pointing to his three hundred knot prayer-rope.

After so many years at the monastery, no one had ever seen him angry. He did not judge others and he never complained. He also had a natural politeness. When he wanted something, he would say, "How are you, Elder?" (He even called the young monks 'Elder'.) "If you love me, bring me this." He was usually in his cassock and cowl at the gate of the monastery, as his job was monastery gatekeeper, and he counselled the pilgrims who came and went.

They wanted to make him *proistamenos*, and in order to avoid this he went and hid in the limekiln. They were looking for him for three days, and finally the abbot spotted him and told him that he had to present himself to the Synaxis and just say 'no,' if he did not want the

---

1   "Εὐλόγησον". This is the same word as the one used for "Forgive me" (see note 2 on p. 130 above); in this case it is the equivalent of "Yes."—ED.

position. When he went in and they offered it to him, he said, "Thank you very much, Elder, may the Panagia reward your efforts. Do you need anything else?... Your blessing," and left. Someone asked him if he regretted not becoming *proistamenos*, to which he firmly answered, "No, I am glad my signature doesn't appear on any document."

He had gone to Elder Joseph the Hesychast for counsel and would later tell others that he was a holy man, and it was from him that he learned the Jesus prayer. He practiced it, not systematically like others but simply, just making an effort to say it as often as possible.

He gave the following counsel, "My child, you should say the Jesus prayer often, not only during your prayer rule. If at some point you get tired, you should chant it in the plagal of the first tone for a while and afterwards start saying it noetically again. And when you go up the stairs, you should say 'Lord Jesus Christ have mercy on me' on every step."

When he got old, the monk in charge of the elderly came to care for him. First the monk cleaned out Elder Evdokimus' cell, emptying it of all the useless things, then he organized it and closed the window. When he brought the elder back to the cell, Evdokimus asked, "But, Father, when will I return to my own cell?" He believed that they had moved him over to another cell, saying, "I haven't laid down in fifty years."

Elder Evdokimus had taken care of many elders in their last years, and had collected a bag full of eyeglasses. The monk in charge of the elderly said, "You have me, the wretched one, to give you a glass of water. I wonder if anyone will take care of me when I'm old." The elder answered peacefully, "Do not worry, Father; God will provide for you as He has provided for me. I have taken care of seven elders in their last years, and God did not leave me. Neither will He leave you."

The monk in charge of the elderly was about to be tonsured in the great schema and announced it to Elder Evdokimus, who was very pleased and blessed him. The younger monk asked him for some counsel, and the elder said to him, "Read two chapters of the New Testament every day. Two chapters. Don't forget them. You should do the Supplication service and the Salutations to the Theotokos, and the prayer-rope. You should work at the Jesus prayer until you hear a voice coming from inside you when you say 'Lord Jesus Christ,' saying 'What do you want?', then you say 'have mercy on me.' If you do not hear the voice, you are not advancing." The elder lived this voice. He also said, "You should not climb a single stair in the monastery without saying the Jesus prayer."

The fathers and the abbot loved him and during his last days they came by to see him every night. He was covered with a heavy woolen blanket, and when he was tired he would pop his head out from under it and say with simplicity, "Father Evdokimus wants quiet now, if you love me...", and cover himself again.

He obeyed the monk in charge of the elderly. He allowed him to wash his body for the first time. Then he said, "My body hasn't seen water for fifty years." He never grumbled or complained, nor did he ever say "Oh, I am in pain!" He was always grateful and glorified God. He would say, "Glory to Thee, O God. We have everything here. In the city hospitals you'll see people without hands and feet, but as for us, we have everything."

The monk in charge of the elderly took care of him, and Elder Evdokimus would say:

"May the Panagia reward you for your labor. Glory to Thee, O God! Everything is good, everything is plentiful. We are having a good time."

"If we are having a good time here, Elder, what will we have when we are there?"[2]

"Here is good, and there is better."

"How are you so sure we will be saved?"

"Father, how could I not be certain? We came here for our salvation. We have struggled for fifty years. If I find myself in a difficult situation, I will call the elder, Saint Paul, and tell him, 'Elder, I've served you for half a century; will you not help me now?'"

Elder Evdokimus was certain that he would be heard. He told the monk that took care of the elderly, "Don't be discouraged, Elder, our elder (Saint Paul) won't abandon us." Before his last days he would

---

2   I.e., in the next life.—TRANS

occasionally go to the hospital. One time the abbot of the monastery visited him there and asked him:

"How are you? Are you well? Do you lack anything?"

"No, glory be to God. I only lack the spiritual."

In his final days he made a detailed confession and communed every day. On his last day, before the service, he had his gaze fixed upward and was not speaking. The monk in charge of the elderly asked him if he was seeing something, and with his overflowing humor he answered, without turning to look at him:

"Not yet; I will tell you later."

The monk again asked, "You seem heavy. Are you perhaps departing?"

"No, man... I would tell you if that were the case."

"Should we bring Holy Communion for you now?"

"After the liturgy is over!"

During the Doxology, the monk went to see him. He felt an indescribable joy, which increased by degrees the nearer he came to the elder's cell. Silence reigned, and when he entered, he saw Elder Evdokimus departed. His soul had flown toward his desired Lord and there was a wide smile on his face. It was the sixteenth of March 1987, the fourth Sunday of Lent, the Sunday of Saint John Climacus, and Elder Evdokimus had completed his seventy-seventh year. They performed his funeral that same afternoon.

May we have his blessing. Amen.

Elder Theodosios of Saint Paul's

Elder Theodosius of Saint Paul's

Father Theodosius of Saint Paul's, born Theodore Antonatos, was born in the village of Atalanti in the region of Locris on March 1st, 1901. He studied at the Business School and, for as long as he was in the world, was occupied with business. He did not have any relationship with the church or with ecclesiastical life, being almost completely opposed to all such things. Wanting to increase business, he acquainted himself with a group of spiritualists, and, indeed, his profits increased.

At the time, a French woman had published a book in France titled "A Month Among the Men," which was disrespectful towards Mount Athos.[1] As it had a large circulation, someone discovered it and, unfortunately, translated it into Greek. A newspaper, which Theodore read religiously, published it in serial format. After reading a few parts, being the restless spirit that he was, he felt curiosity and a desire to visit Mt Athos. He thought: "This Frenchwoman wrote so many things that if even half of them are true, the Holy Mountain must, indeed, be noteworthy. I will go."

After a few days there was a meeting of his spiritualist group and he attended. But for some strange reason there were no revelations from the spirits. They invoked them and invoked them, but nothing. Then they heard a voice say, "If Theodore does not change his mind about the decision he made, we cannot say anything!" This only in-

---

1   *Un Mois Chez les Hommes* by Maryse Choisy. She later confessed and revealed that what she wrote was a lie, and she had not actually visited the Holy Mountain, but as per usual this was silenced by the media. As a sign of repentance, however, she donated the proceeds of the book to a charitable institution in France.

creased his stubbornness, however, and he scheduled his visit to the Holy Mountain.

He arrived on Mount Athos on the eve of the feast of the Dormition, and following the masses of pilgrims, he went to Iviron. He attended the vigil and it made quite an impression on him, but it did not spiritually change him. Then he visited Saint Paul's, and there something happened inside him. He decided to go to confession and then announced his desire to remain to the spiritual father of the monastery, Father Ignatius (disciple of the well-known Father Ignatius the Spiritual Father). The fathers accepted him, and he became part of the monastery. On the nineteenth of February 1936, he was tonsured a monk with the name Theodosius.

When he was a young monk, Father Theodosius, wanting spiritual benefit, visited the abbot of the monastery of Grigoriou, Father Athanasius, who was renowned for his virtue. The abbot gave him valuable counsel concerning the monastic life and before leaving said to him, "If you want to become a good monk, you should read Saint Ephraim the Syrian. You should always have him under your pillow." Indeed, he began to read Saint Ephraim every day and reaped great spiritual fruit from it. Father Theodosius loved Saint Ephraim very much but became convinced by the humble expressions that Saint Ephraim used to refer to himself (for example, that he was a sinner, worthy of hell, et cetera.) that Saint Ephraim was, indeed, in hell. He suffered greatly on this account, and since he loved him, he prayed on his prayer-rope for God to remove him from hell.

One day, when the abbot had him do the customary reading in the refectory, he read something related to Saint Ephraim, his life or some encomium, and was surprised to see that Saint Ephraim was not only not in hell but also a great saint. He started weeping from joy and excitement, and the reading was interrupted.

Father Theodosius worked hard. He stayed up all night to organize the monastery's library. He also created an ossuary with icons. He was careful in his studies and wrote spiritual books. Many of the saints' lives and patristic texts in the monastery were written by him.

Father Theodosius fought the devil intensely, since he had been mixed up in spiritualism as a layman. The devil attacked him fiercely, and they fought in hand-to-hand combat. He confessed these attacks of temptation to the abbot and having confidence in himself said, "If he dares to come back, you'll see what I'll do to him." The same night, the tempter came as usual, Father Theodosius rushed on him manically, grabbed him by the cheek with one hand, and tried to throw him down with the other. But in a little while he felt the opponent overcoming him. And so, seeing the insufficiency of his own strength, he called upon Christ and the Virgin Mary, and immediately the temptation disappeared, not being able to endure the power of the Name.

He then ran to the Abbot and confessed, "What I said earlier, that 'If he comes, you'll see what I'll do to him,' was my pride." He learned by experience that demons are conquered by humility and divine power.

He narrated: "One night, while I was writing about spiritualism, someone knocked on my windowpane very forcefully, so much so that it was about to break. I looked through the glass and saw a shadow. I said, 'Leave, in the name of Christ' constantly making the sign of the cross on the window. A little while later I saw a shadow, like an astronaut, moving away."

Another time the following happened, as he explained: "One night, Father Gerasimus from Little Saint Anne's came to my cell.

'When did you come? I didn't notice you.'

'Oh, this afternoon. I learned that you are publishing a book.'

'Yes. About spiritualism.'

Then Father Gerasimus said to me:

'Ninety-nine percent of what the mediums say is true. One percent is lies, and that one percent invalidates the ninety-nine percent.'

'What you said is beautiful. I'll add it to the book, but what is the source?'

'The Spiritual Exercises.'

When he left my cell, I opened Spiritual Exercises, found it immediately, and copied it into the book. When I finished the first draft of the work and was ready to send it to the typist, I had a sudden urge to double-check the Spiritual Exercises' page where that passage was written, of which Father Gerasimus had told me. I searched the entire book three times and did not find it anywhere, so I got up, went to Little Saint Anne's, found Father Gerasimus, and said: 'When you came to the monastery, you told me such and such. Now I cannot find the passage in the book. What's going on?' He replied, 'I did not come to Saint Paul's. I haven't been there in a very long time. And I did not say any such thing to you.'

I was speechless. Had I truly been deceived by the devil to such a degree? Then I thought that, had I written that, it would have been a great disaster, as whoever read the book would think: 'Since ninety-nine percent of what they say is true, what does the one percent matter? I'll go to a medium.'
When I had prepared the book about spiritualism, I was doing the final edits in order to send to the publisher in the morning. There were still four pages left to finish, and suddenly I felt the devil next to me. I felt a shiver go through my whole body, and the temptation was telling me to stop. I said, 'No, I will finish and then I'll stop', and I continued to write, crying, 'My Christ, help me.' When I was finished, I lay down for a bit. In a few minutes I was completely debilitated by the devil. I couldn't even scream. Only my mind and reason were able to function. Then I remembered abba Isaac's words, 'Only the spirit of God can drive away the spirit of the evil one,' and I began praying fervently. In a little while the devil left, and I was free.'"

He also told the following: "One night I felt my bed shaking violently. I thought that we were experiencing a strong earthquake, and with a seismic rift of such magnitude, the buildings would collapse and the monastery would be destroyed. As soon as it stopped I went outside and into the church, where the sacristan was lighting the vigil lamps. I said, 'I think there was an earthquake. Did you feel anything?' He answered in the negative, and as I thought it was strange, I asked another monk, who also replied 'no.' In the morning I asked all the fathers, and all of them answered that they did not feel the earthquake. Then I thought, 'Oh what Satan does to me!'"

On the twenty-ninth of September of every year, Father Theodosius went to the feast at the cell of the "Gobdelades" ("of Saint Govdelas"). Saints Gobdelas and Casdoa are wonderworkers and had performed a great miracle at the monastery of Koutloumousi.

There was an icon of them there and the monastery used to do a vigil on their feastday. Father Theodosius had a health problem, eczema in his hands, and when it flared up it looked so awful that people were too disgusted to kiss his hand in blessing. One year, by God's providence, he forgot and did not go to the feast of Saint Govdelas. When he remembered, he felt great sorrow, weeping, and repeating, "How could I miss the vigil of the Saints?!" A tear fell on his hands, and they were healed from the eczema. He considered it a miracle of the saints.

There was a period during which Father Theodosius was sick for a long time. He had a fever of 106°F and could not even stand on his feet. During that time the relics of the Neomartyr Pachomius came. As soon as he found out he invoked the saint, and immediately he became well, the fever left him, and he went down and venerated the holy relics.

Since he was educated and active, he helped his monastery a great deal, primarily with administrative matters. He became the representative and superintendent of the monastery at the Holy Community in Karyes. When he saw the restaurant cooking meat on a fasting day, he threw gasoline into the pan.

His opinion held weight at the monastery's synaxis and his opinion prevailed, as all the fathers recognized his worth and respected him.

There were very few places where Elder Theodosius did not help. There was a period during which he resigned, both as *proistamenos* and from the monastery's office, and during that period he ran the refectory and went to tend to the olive trees. He was extremely energetic. When he was seventy-eight years old, he took over the cell of Saint Spyridon, and after the service he would take his bag and go water the olives, even in the midst of heat waves if needed. He was indefatigable.

He had great love and tried to bring comfort and peace to the fathers. When he was head of the refectory (they did not have refrigerators at the time), he made sure to put the watermelons in water so that they would get somewhat cold in order to refresh the fathers. He was always trying to do the best to make the fathers comfortable, basing his actions on Saint Theodore the Studite. For this reason he often went to help out in the kitchen.

There was a period during which he served as the monastery's monitor. Every night, after compline, he would walk barefoot outside the cells. If he heard conversations inside, he would not say anything, but during the morning service he would say to the monks who were talking after compline, "Make sure this does not happen again." He had discretion.

In his last days, as he lay on a bed with a prayer-rope, someone asked him, "What are you thinking? How do you feel?" to which he answered, "I am thinking that I will go to the Lord, and I feel very happy." Indeed, his face was joyful, and two days later, on the fourth of July, at the age of eighty-six, he fell asleep in the Lord.

He was extremely possessionless. This hidden virtue was revealed after his death, when the fathers could not even find clothes to dress him, so one monk gave a cassock, another a cowl, and another some pants.

May we have his blessing. Amen.

Abbot Evdokimus of Xenophontos

The most holy abbot of Xenophontos Evdokimus was born in the town of Amphicleia (Drymia) in the region of Locris in 1906. He was born to Demetris and Chrysoula Skouphas and named Eustace. There is no information regarding his pre-monastic life, because it was not easy to get the elder to speak about himself. He confessed and went to church, ended his military service with the rank of sergeant, and when he decided to become a monk, he first went to the Monastery of Olympiotissa. He was not at peace there, however, as the monastery had many visitors, including women. He then considered becoming a monk on Athos and asked his spiritual father. Unfortunately, he dissuaded him, telling him that all the criminals went to Athos.

The young Eustace, however, was not influenced, and following the divine voice that called him to dedicate himself to God, he and a fellow soldier came to the Holy Mountain in 1929, at the age of twenty-three. Apparently he did not know any monks and he had no preference as to where he should live. At that time the monasteries were full to capacity and did not easily accept young men coming to them to become monks. He first went to Xeropatomou, but they rejected him, and then he went to Xenophontos. Though they did not have a need for new monks, they saw that he was strong and muscular and considered him useful for hard labor. They accepted him and asked if he could help in the kitchen. They gave him a cassock and he stayed there for five years, serving in the monastery. He arrived on February 4, 1929, and after a one-year novitiate, he was tonsured a monk on the sixteenth of March 1930. He was given the name Evdokimus ("approved" or "successful"), and this name suited him perfectly since he succeeded in all the different obediences that he was assigned. After the first five years, his next five years were spent as sacristan. He would wake up very early and prepare the church for services, and he held onto this good habit (of going to church before anyone else) for his entire monastic life.

According to the old order that existed in the monasteries, he went through all the different work positions. He confessed his sins often and thoroughly to Father Polycarp who was extremely virtuous. He would later say, "My daily confession helped save my exactness in monasticism."

Indeed, he was very exact in his monastic practices and once, when they asked him if monks are allowed to swim in the sea, he answered: "In our years (when he was a young monk) even looking at the sea was considered a sin."

He worked on the mountain for quite a few years as the director of the foresters and woodcutters. Apart from mules, the monastery also had oxen with which they transported the felled trees. It was extremely laborious work, but Father Evdokimus was the first to jump in and the best at the job. He also served as bullkeeper . He was a violent monk[1] and always said the Jesus prayer as he worked.

One year there was a heavy winter storm and he and a lay worker who was helping were stranded on the mountain. They watched over the bulls and stayed in a house without a church in a place called Zahara. Their supplies ran out and someone had to go and get food. The worker volunteered to go, but Father Evdokimus would not let him: "You have a wife and kids; I have no such responsibilities: if I am lost, no one will mourn me. I will go." He started off in the morning, buried in the snow, taking whatever he could carry on his back, and, through great effort, was back by dusk. The worker was looking at the road all day, and when he at last saw him, he was extremely happy. It looked as if the monk were carrying a lantern, but when he came closer, the worker saw that he was not holding any light but that it was his face shining. The worker told him this, and Father Evdokimus,

---

1   See Matthew 11:12: "the kingdom Heaven suffereth violence, and the violent take it by force."—ED.

Abbot Evdokimus of Xenophontos

not paying any attention, replied, "Be quiet. Next you'll be telling me that I'm a saint."

For a period of time, from December 1, 1945 to April 13, 1946, he voluntarily left the monastery. The reason is unknown, and he quickly returned.

Later, a problem arose in the administration of the monastery, and no one could be settled in as abbot. In a one-year period they had seven different abbots, and after the seventh stepped down, they finally settled on Father Evdokimus who until then was a simple monk working on the mountain. They had previously made him *proistamenos* and he had begun to put the monastery in order, so they now proposed to ordain him a priest and then make him abbot. He did not initially accept, but the then abbot of Dionysiou Gabriel, whom he admired and to whom he went for counsel, managed to convince him to accept. And so, on the fifteenth of November 1953, he was ordained a priest and the next month, on the fourteenth of December 1953, he was enthroned as abbot.

After he was elected abbot, someone mocked him, saying, "Art thou he that should come, or do we look for another?" (Mt. 11:3). He did not answer but he thought to himself, "I'll take care of you." This monk was the representative of the monastery and he both "bound and loosed."[2] He was the reason none of the abbots could settle in. Father Evdokimus removed him from the position of representative and the monastery found peace.

It seems that Father Evdokimus was the right man for the job because he helped his monastery. He later said with humility: "Maybe I did not help the monastery spiritually, but I did help it materially." He was an example for all the monks,and was always first for both work and church. Since the fathers were few in number and advanced in age, Father Evdokimus became baker, cook, sacristan, and officiating priest. He did not stop at all. His sacrificed himself and deprived himself of sleep in order to manage all the different tasks. Being abbot did not change his behavior. His cell was simple, and he lived with the other priests in a wing close to the chapel of Saint Euphemia. When

---

2   That is, he had great power.—ED.

someone came to the abbot for business, he would receive him in his cell. In all his years and in all the different phases of his monastic life he held this principle: whenever anyone knocked at the door, whatever the time, even if he was sleeping, he would jump up and open the door immediately. He would say, "I can sleep later, but will I be able to find my brother later?" He was like a mother that took care of everyone. Troubled monks from other monasteries found refuge near him, and the monastery's workers served him with love. The door of his cell was never locked. It was open to everyone.

He always wore the same simple, slightly dirty monastic clothes. When his shoes fell apart he would not buy new ones but patch them up himself, and for this reason some people derisively called him "tsarouchas."[3] He never embraced grandeur and was not impressed by luxurious vestments. He rarely wore the abbot's cloak and once, when they brought it to him, he jokingly said, "I'm not cold." When he saw a certain monk wearing an official wide-sleeved cassock, he told him, "Ah, my poor man (his usual expression), are you an archimandrite of the Patriarchate or an administrator of Vatopedi?"

As an abbot he fought with all his strength to help the monastery economically, as its needs were many and great. In order not to waste money unnecessarily he went to Thessaloniki himself when supplies were necessary and ate the cheapest food in the cheapest restaurants. He did not go about officiating like an abbot but acted like a simple monk.

There were times when, after returning to Ouranoupolis,[4] he would go back to the monastery by foot, preferring to walk the seven or eight hours rather than pay for a ticket for the boat. One time he went out to Thessaloniki and returned carrying much money with him. He missed the boat at Ouranoupolis and the local boatmen asked for twelve drachmas to take him to Xenophontos. He told them ten. They could not agree, and he returned to the monastery on foot in

3   A *tsarouchi* is an old-fashioned traditional Greek shoe with a pom-pom. It was part of the soldier's outfit in the 19th century but by the 20th century it had fallen out of fashion and was only worn by farmers and shepherds.—TRANS
4   The port city at which one arrives to get paperwork, a ticket, and a boat to travel on to the Holy Mountain.—TRANS

order to not pay the two extra drachmas. He considered the money and property of the monastery sacred; they belonged to the patron saint and he was afraid to spend it carelessly, as he felt that he was a servant of the monastery.

He also constructed new buildings and built separators between the wings for fire protection. He increased the monastery's possessions, turning the seventeen mules that he found upon his ascendency into seventy. He was abbot and yet worked like a hired worker. Once, a worker was making raki[5] and the roof caught on fire. He yelled for the abbot, who came running. Abbot Evdokimus did not call anyone else, putting the fire out himself and telling the worker not to worry. He never told anyone of this. Whenever he returned to the monastery, he would look in the storage room to see if anything was missing. He did not buy fish. Sometimes Italian fishermen came with inflatable boats and filled his storerooms with grouper. They also made salted grouper and the abbot gave them *krasoraki* (a mix of raki and wine) in return. He was good at being in charge, even if some administrators considered him tight-fisted. One of these administrators would cook his own meals in his cell. The abbot figured it out and said: "My poor man, the smells have made it all the way to the kitchen," to which the monk replied: "If you put food like this in the refectory, I'll stop cooking in my cell." The abbot then responded, "If I put such foods in the refectory, we will bankrupt the monastery."

Abbot Evdokimus was intelligent, quick-witted, fair, and direct, in both word and action. Once, someone stole some wood, and he, following the tracks of the pack animals, found the stolen wood. He did not ask for anything or chide the thief, but only told him, "Blessed man, why didn't you tell me that you needed wood so that I could give you some?"

One time a merchant came to buy the monastery's bulls. Thinking wickedly and in order to profit illegally, he shut the bulls in the stable for two days without any food or water, and then brought them to the monastery to be weighed at night.[6] When the abbot saw them, he understood what had happened. He called a worker and at midnight

---

5   A sweet alcoholic beverage.—TRANS
6   The price was determined by the weight.—TRANS

they fed the bulls bran with salt. The bulls naturally got thirsty, and when they brought them to water, they drank generously and came back to their normal weight. When the merchant saw the bulls with bloated bellies, he said, "Until today I had fooled everyone, but I could not fool this monk." The abbot did this in order to save the merchant's soul from the weight of the sin and also because he could not tolerate injustice against the monastery.

He sold a field that the monastery owned, and the lawyers offered to give him a share of the sale price. He responded, "The price I asked is for my monastery. I do not want anything for myself. I am a monk, and monks do not own anything."

Abbot Evdokimus did a great deal of secret almsgiving. When he went out he took a full wallet and a block of receipts. Whenever a poor person asked him for money he gave it, and when there were larger needs, he would cut them a receipt, saying, "Return it when you're able." He made packages with food and provisions, took them with him, and distributed them to poor families. He helped a poor student from the villages of Halkidiki go to college. Today he is a university professor and grateful to abbot Evdokimus.

Amongst his virtues, one that stood out was his perfect sense of detachment. He did not have any communication with his biological relatives, so much so that the one time he sent them a letter regarding an urgent matter, they did not even know from whom it was.

In his dogmatic convictions he was a guardian of the exactness of Orthodox tradition. Several abbots ceased commemorating the Patriarch for a time, and his monastery agreed to do the same. After a period the other monasteries resumed commemoration, but he did not. The Patriarchal Exarchate, then presided by bishop Maximus of Stavroupoli, came to discuss this with Elder Evdokimus, and after the abbot explained the reasons for which he ceased commemoration in the first place, the president of the Exarchate asked him:

"Holy Abbot, how many monks do you have here?"

"How many that are here to eat, or how many that are here to work?"

"How can you speak like that?" the bishop angrily responded. "Do you not know that I can take away the (abbot's) staff you're holding?"

The abbot then offered him the staff and said, "Take it. I did not come here to be abbot. I came to save my soul."

And so, on the third of March 1974, by Patriarchal decree, he was removed from the office of abbot. The then political administrator of Athos, Mr. D. Kriekoukias later issued document number Φ26/12/15 6.1974, which commanded that "Abbot Evdokimus leave the holy monastery of his repentance, since he insists on his own spiritual positions."

During this period between his deposition and exile, he continued to help the monastery with different jobs, as he was a man of great bodily stamina. At that time the monastery did not have a priest for the daily services, so Father Joannikius from the Skete of Xenophontos celebrated the daily services while Father Evdokimus officiated on Sundays and feastdays. One time he was in Thessaloniki on business and arrived in Ouranoupolis on Saturday morning. Since there was no transportation, he walked to the monastery (an eight-hour journey), celebrated vigil on Saturday night, and liturgy on Sunday morning as normal. He was over seventy years old at the time.

He loved the monastery of his repentance very much; it was an earthly paradise for him. He felt like Adam, who kept and cultivated paradise but was destined to be exiled. He found himself exiled on October 24th, 1977, three years after the written order. He was not saddened much over losing the abbotship, but he suffered greatly over being exiled from his monastery for which he had given so much sweat, and in which he had lived for forty-eight years (twenty-two as abbot).

With bitterness and pain, he moved to the neighboring monastery of Docheiariou and became a disciple to a simple monk. He obeyed him, and even when the monk would correct him about something publicly, he would humbly say, "Bless," revealing the depth of his humility.

In the beginning of his exile, in order to soften his agony, he would take the boat to Daphne every day, wanting to see his monastery even from afar. When he saw it, he would weep and say, "Adam sat outside

Paradise...”[7] Other times, to joke away his pain, he would pretend that he did not know and ask, "Which monastery is that?"

Once, while conversing with a layman at Daphne, he found out that the man gave eighty thousand drachmas to the previous sacristan of Docheiariou for the monastery's needs as he had great love for the Panagia Quick-to-Hear (Γοργοεπήκοος), whose miraculous icon was housed at the monastery. The discerning elder did not say anything so as not to scandalize the benefactor, but rather he did the following: returning to the monastery he found the former sacristan and told him: "Father, there is talk at Daphne about someone giving you eighty thousand drachmas for the monastery. What will happen if the abbot finds out? If you want, hold on to five thousand drachmas and give me the rest so that I can give it to the abbot; the responsibility will mine." Indeed, the monk gave him the money and Elder Evdokimus gave it to the abbot saying, "Holy abbot, take this money for the monastery. Someone gave it to me. And if you find out that there was more to begin with, I was the one that took it." And so, with his discerning intervention, the matter was set in order. He was a man "for edification, and not for destruction" (2 Cor. 10:8)

Many times during his forced exile he felt the sense of injustice almost choking him, and his mind told him to protest the decree. Then, one day while he was reading the Philokalia, he found a passage that made him resign from every effort to do so, going as far as to burn his correspondence with some of his old enemies and forgiving them. He then felt very light-hearted and joyful.

An acquaintance of his, a worker, offered to draw up a contract and deed him some land outside Athos, on which the former abbot could gather the money to build a monastery. He did not accept, saying, "There may be land elsewhere, but there is no Holy Mountain elsewhere."

He preferred to remain an exile on the Holy Mountain, to live in obedience to a simple monk, and from abbot be demoted to sacristan, and all that with joy. He would say, "Being a sacristan is the best job, because you are constantly with the saints, lighting their vigil lamps."

---

7   The beginning of a hymn from the Triodion.—ED.

During a certain feast, the *typikaris*[58] told him to light the candles on the church chandelier, which Father Evdokimus began to do. Suddenly and loudly, in front of everyone, the *typikaris* said, "You old *tsaroucha*, did I tell you to light them now?" The former abbot silently accepted the insult, obeyed, and told himself, "Patience, *Evdokime*."

When Docheiariou became a coenobium, the former abbot had a distinguished place in it. When the current abbot of Docheiariou would ask his opinion on a matter, he would do so humbly and respectfully, calling him "holy abbot" and doing a prostration before him. His counsels concerned practical monastic matters, for example, telling the abbot to accommodate the fathers and put a little oil in their food when they were engaged in heavy labor. For himself, he only requested not to go to the refectory but to eat in his cell. He did not do this out of idiosyncrasy but because one meal a day was enough for him. He would always come down for the services and vigils and, when the typikaris told him so, would chant as much his voice allowed. He also advised them to clear the area around the monastery of shrubbery so that if the forest caught fire the monastery would not burn, and if the monastery caught fire the forest would be spared. They gave him the task of monastery's forester, and despite his age he cleared all the paths to the neighboring monasteries and to Karyes.

This crude and unsophisticated bullkeeper had a certain spiritual nobility and sensitivity. No one ever saw him angry, and he was always friendly and pleasant with all the monks. He was never offended by anyone and would counsel others not to delay but immediately reconcile and do a prostration to each other whenever misunderstandings occurred. He avoided idle chatter and the judging of one's fellow man. He was quiet and terse, speaking very little. He was not verbally gifted, teaching more by example. What he did say, however, came from experience, and his word held weight. He always lived in obscurity, in the margins, desiring to go by unnoticed. He was so hesychastic that later, when roads were built, he would go hide in the forest whenever he heard a car. He was characteristically abrupt and hard on himself. In outward appearance he was always unkempt, with old and slightly

---

8   A monk in charge of the order of the service.—TRANS.

dirty cassocks, but internally he was spotless, and his eyes revealed sympathy and compassion. He had a thick beard,and his face was sunburned and furrowed with wrinkles. His hair was whitish-blonde and receding, and always loose and scruffy.

He was possessionless. He spent his pension money buying oil for the vigil lamps and juices and sweets for the monks of his monastery, which he himself distributed during work-time to refresh the laboring fathers. From the jetty he would go straight to the fields like a child and hand them out himself, so that in this way he could participate in the work that was going on.

Even though he gave sweets to others, he never ate them himself, saying, "We old monks didn't learn to eat sweets, and if we saw half a loukoumi[9] thrown out, we felt sorrow and considered it a sin. Today I see piles of sweets, and the fathers both eat them and throw them away with ease."

He did not ask anything for himself, nor did he have a complaint against anyone. He would tell the cook not to cook anything specifically for him but only to send him a little broth from the other monks' food. They would also bring him a glass of wine which strengthened him, as in his old age he was worn out. When the monastery gatekeeper wanted to offer him some raki, he would say "3 to 1," that is, to dilute one part raki with three parts water.

During Great Lent he fasted three days a week, not eating anything from Monday to Wednesday. On Wednesday he would receive the Presanctified Gifts and afterward eat bread and olives. On Thursday he would abstain from food again, and on Friday he would receive the Presanctified Gifts and then again eat bread and olives. On the weekends he would eat food with oil. He repeated this fasting schedule every week during Great Lent.

He cell was very poor and unkempt, just as he was. Once some monks came and cleaned it without his knowledge, and when he saw it, he laughed and said, "You should have only bothered to do this once: after my death. Why do you tire yourselves pointlessly?"

---

9   Commonly known to Westerners as Turkish Delight.—TRANS.

He had three blankets stitched together for warmth. He attached one end to the wall so that they would not fall off when he slept and leave him cold. He slept in his clothes: "I only take off my shoes," he would say. Next to his cell was a chapel of the Three Hierarchs, small and prayerful. Every day he lit the votive lamps, keeping them perpetually lit with very large flames.

Even though he loved animals, he greatly disliked cats. If he saw a monk petting a cat, he would say, "Don't, my poor man, it is not right to pet cats. They're too soft." While the cats slept without a care in the world, when they would hear his footsteps and his cane on the stairs, they would jump up in terror and run to hide. It was a spectacle that provoked laughter amongst the monks. Once he went down to the port and there was a cat at the edge of the jetty. The former abbot walked towards it with his cane and the cat, not being able to escape, fell into the sea and had to swim to shore. He laughed as he recounted, "It preferred to commit suicide."

In the last years of his life, Father Evdokimus saw a vision. While he was lying down, someone showed him all of his sins, as in an outline, and a voice said to him: "Your sins have not been completely washed away." The former abbot replied, asking, "And how will they be written off?" and the voice said, "With the Jesus prayer." From that moment on he began to say the Jesus prayer effortlessly within himself.

He always held a thirty-three-knot prayer-rope, both during services and outside the church, and would constantly say the prayer. Usually his small prayer-rope was knotted, not woven in the normal manner, and sometimes with white thread.

He was first in church for the services. He would stand in the first seat on the right of the nave holding his prayer-rope, saying the Jesus prayer and moving his head. On account of his age he ceased to officiate at Divine Liturgy, which was the custom of the older Athonites, but he still put on his stole and did the daily services when the priest was absent.

The following are amongst his stereotypical teachings, "poor in words, but rich in spiritual depth": "Man's mind is the fastest thing in the world. We have to say the prayer constantly to stop it from going where it shouldn't."

"If a monk has lived uprightly and struggled when he was young, then his old age is all mystagogy and pleasure, like a loaded ship that finally arrives at harbor. If, however, he lives carelessly, then woe to him."

Wanting to highlight the value of experience, he would tell younger monks, "Tell me everything you know, and I'll tell you everything I've suffered."

Regarding those who were excessively distracted by work he would say, "My poor man, work never ends. We end. Even Methuselah who lived for so long left unfinished work behind when he died."

He was saddened that men did not live righteously and weren't grateful to God. He would characteristically say, "What do I do for you, Lord, which you do not see, and what do I prepare for you which you do not know?" When he mentioned God, he would piously refer to him as "the holy God," and when someone asked for his blessing, he would bless him saying, "May God forgive you."

Many times, during discussions in which he mentioned the saints, he would feel prayerful, and his eyes would fill with tears. He would say, "I've read the *Philoalia*, the *Sayings of the Desert Fathers*, the *Ladder of Divine Ascent*, and other books, but nothing captivates and delights my soul like the lives of the saints." Towards the end of his life he wept much more.

Every single day, until the day when he was no longer able to leave his bed, he would go down to the church when the first bell rang, thirty minutes before the beginning of the service. He venerated the icons and took his seat. During the daily services he would leave before the end, but on Sunday he would stay until the end to commune. As the Communion Hymn was being chanted, he would venerate the icons, then go into the altar and put on his stole, which he held in his arm until that point. He would ask for the abbot's forgiveness, and then commune as the last priest.

In the last months of his life, the monastery of Xenophontos asked him to come back. He rejected their offer saying, "I've lived here with these fathers for so many years, and we've never exchanged an unbiblical word. How can I now leave them and come back? If you'd asked a long time ago I would have returned, but now I have arrived at the end." And so he enjoyed the full spiritual rewards of his exile.

On the week of Pentecost he got sick and the fathers wanted to take him to the hospital in Thessaloniki, but he told them, "You won't make it in time." He also stopped drinking the little glass of wine that the cook sent him, and as he had said long ago, "You should know that when I can no longer drink the wine, I will die." He told the fathers, "When I die, do not look for anything in my cell. Whatever I own will be in my pockets." Indeed, nothing was found in his cell except the cassock that he was wearing.

A certain monk asked him: "Elder, you've lived on the Holy Mountain for so many years. What do you take away from the experience? What is the meaning of monastic life?" The elder answered: "Humility."

For the last three days of his life he did not eat anything but only drank water. They did the service of Unction for him, and before it had finished, he had peacefully fallen asleep in the Lord. It was Sunday, the first of July 1990. They invited Alexius, the abbot of Xenophontos, to officiate at his funeral. The day after his death, they received a note from the Ecumenical Patriarch lifting his punishment.

The former abbot Evdokimus died far from home, exiled, slandered, misunderstood, and scorned. No one outside of the monastery which took him in as an exile took any interest in him. He was forgotten by all. He had suffered in life, being "humbled exceedingly." He had labored greatly for his monastery, and struggled as a monk. May "the holy God," as he would call Him, in His righteousness and mercy grant him the place that he deserves in His kingdom. Amen.

May we have his blessing. Amen.

The Mysterious Recluse Herodion

Elder Herodion of Kapsala was born in Ordarsest, Romania, in 1904. His parents, Peter and Helen Mantouf, named him John.

He came to the Holy Mountain and became a monk at the Dionysian[1] cell of the Entrance of the Theotokos but later lived in different cells, mostly in the area of Kapsala. On October 28, 1964, he moved to the cell of Saint Demetrios in Kapsala, and the last years of his life were solitary, harsh, and comfortless. He had a cistern in his cell from which he drew water, and when a mouse fell in one day, he refused to leave his cell to get water from elsewhere. Elder Macarius, his neighbor, brought him water from that day on. He did not gather supplies, shop for necessities, make handiwork to sell, or cultivate a garden. God, who provides for the ravens, provided for Elder Herodion as well.

When someone came to visit, he would open the door, poke his head out a little, and begin to speak, as he knew Romanian, Russian, and Greek. He said many incoherent things, telling people that he had authority over the sun and the rain, et cetera. Amidst the nonsense, however, Elder Herodion would say certain things which would remain in his visitors' minds. He would speak of personal things concerning the visitor, things that no one could have known. After they left, some would wonder what this indescribable mystery named Elder Herodion was. Was he a prophet, a madman, deluded, or something else?

Three things, however, were clear beyond any doubt to whoever went to visit Elder Herodion of Kapsala. The first was his peaceful,

---

1   One of the cells not far from Karyes under the Chilandari Monastery.—TRANS.

sweet, joyful face with its ascetic paleness and yellow, transparent, quince-colored tinge. Even though it was unwashed, dirty, and leathered, the sight of his face did not repel but on the contrary made one feel drawn to him.

The second was his great self-denial. He was well over eighty years old, and yet he frequently went completely without food for days, as he lacked even the most basic necessities. He lived in a derelict hut which hardly protected him from the elements, as the roof leaked and there was no heating. 1986 was a difficult year, with a harsh winter and long frosts, and his survival is not humanly explicable, especially given the fact that he walked around his cell barefoot and did not have a bed. He was always standing or leaning against the edge of a counter which was full of useless old garbage.

When he was a young monk, a cell in the area of Provata caught fire, and they unjustly blamed him for causing it. Some lay workers, beleving the false rumors, beat him severely. After this, when asked why he did not light a fire in the winter, he would say: "Lest I burn down Kapsala." Perhaps he simply set a rule for himself to never light a fire.

They once asked him what he does when he gets cold, to which he answered: "I go to Sinai and warm up" (perhaps meaning mentally), or "A monk that truly struggles is like a man that has the month of May inside of him. He never gets cold." Elder Païsius would say that "the fact that he stays in his cell with such deprivation means that he has consolation from God."

The third was his clairvoyance and foreknowledge. He told many people with what they were struggling before they even opened their mouth. Three fathers from Corfu visited him and he knew where they were from without their telling him. He told another that he had bought a cap and should wear it a few days later when he goes out, and so it happened.

A monk once went to ask him about indecisiveness; he had two thoughts (*logismoi*) and knew not which to follow. Before he had asked, Elder Herodion told him, "Do not let opinion divide you; *you* should divide it."

Another time, during Great Lent, the same monk felt exhaustion and went to ask the elder if he could break the fast with a

The mysterious recluse Herodion

little oil. Before he had asked, the elder replied, "If you cannot, you should eat a little oil."

Another time also, without being asked, Elder Herodion said to a monk who had the thought to submit himself to Elder Niketas: "Elder Niketas. He needs to know if he is to guide you. Otherwise, better sit in your cell."

He told another monk that at their cell, which was on ground level, he was seeing great balconies looking towards the sea, although their cell did not have any. When they constructed a new building with large balconies, then they remembered what Elder Herodion had said.

In Bourazeri also he said that he was seeing a beautiful large church of the Panagia amidst flowers in the middle of the cell's courtyard, while there was no such thing.[2] Years later, when they built the new church, then the fathers remembered his words.

Two pilgrims went to see him and he started speaking of the one man's problem and what he would face when he went out of the Holy Mountain. The other man then asked him:

"Do you not have anything to say to me?"

"*Your* problem is at Sykia."[3]

The man looked around him but said that he did not see any *sykiá*.

"To get to the Sykia that I mean, you cross the sea."

Still, the man did not understand and left perplexed. As soon as he returned to his house which was in the village Sykia near Corinth, his family had a serious health problem, and then he remembered the words of Elder Herodion.

Once, when Elder Meletius the Romanian had taken him to Saint George to look after him in his old age, a certain monk visited him, along with a young man. As soon as he saw them in the distance (he was sitting by the door with the cats), he shouted in a rage for the young man to stop because he had a machine. Indeed, the youth was holding in his hand a bag which contained

---

2   Although its official status is that of a cell, the Sacred Cell of Saint Nicholas (Bourazeri) is as large as a monastery; hence the courtyard.—ED.

3   Sykia: lit. "the fig-tree."—ED.

a photographic machine. God knows how Elder Herodion saw it. He was also visited by official men, such as the Protos ogf the Holy Mountain and the hieromonk Païsius of Chilandari Monastery.

Elder Herodion used to give one piece of good advice, such as, for instance, "When the monk sits in his cell and does not concern himself with others but prays instead, then the love of God comes into him." Then he would say incoherent things and behave like a fool; and of course no one could ever figure out or come to any conclusion regarding Elder Herodion.

One time two monks visited him. They knocked on the door but he was not answering. They could hear whispering. From a little window they could see him turned towards the wall, motionless, whispering something, and deaf to the outside world. They waited for half an hour, but he was not once distracted from prayer.

Since he was constantly standing, his feet had become swollen and rigid, like unbending columns. He had a large wound, the size of a walnut, under the large toe of one of his feet, which emitted a foul odor. Since he always went around barefoot, it was covered with dirt, so you could not easily see it.

For the last eight days of his life, Elder Herodion did not eat or drink anything. It seems that he had foreseen his death and was preparing. His body had become yellow like a lemon, and when he fell asleep during the Advent Fast, on the twelfth of December 1990, Elder Meletius said that his cell was full of a sweet fragrance.

May God grant rest to his soul and warm him in Paradise now, as he suffered greatly from cold in this vain life.

May we have his blessing. Amen.

Abbot Evthymius of Zographou

Abbot Evthymius of Zographou

Evthymius, the abbot of Zographou, was born on October 10, 1926, in the village of Enchevtsi in the province of Veliko Tarnovo in Bulgaria.[1] He was baptized with the name Bogomil, and from a young age he was distinguished for his intelligence and piety. He finished middle school with the highest possible marks and his father intended to have him succeed him in his business. When Bogomil finished his military service, however, he told his parents that he wanted to become a priest in their village.

He enrolled in seminary, which at that time was at the Chrepish Monastery, and finished in three years with excellent marks. He returned to his village, where everyone expected him to be ordained, as he was universally loved for his meekness, piety, and quiet and kind character, but he first had to find a wife. Since he was inexperienced in such things, he asked a priest friend of his to find him a presbytera.[2] The girl that was selected, however, was unsuitable, so he left his village and worked as a construction worker for the next ten years, from 1951 to 1961. Yet, he retained his piety and principles and remained a faithful child of the Church.

Early in 1962 he decided to become a monk at the Monastery of the Transfiguration (Preobrazhenski Monastery) near Veliko Tarnovo. After the standard period of novitiate, he was tonsured with the name Evthymius, and the very next year he was finally ordained a priest.

When listening to the canon during Matins, he would always cross himself and make a prostration during every troparion. When some

1 Modern-day Enchovtsi in the municipality of Tryavna.—TRANS.
2 Priest's (presbyter's) wife.—TRANS.

seminarians visited and asked for a blessing, he blessed them, but then, though a hieromonk himself, he took and kissed their hands.

In 1964, they sent him to be the daily celebrant in the nearby women's monastery of Sts. Peter and Paul. The monastery had been destroyed by a fire, and Father Evthymius worked right alongside the sisters to rebuild it. It was difficult manual labor, as they even made their own bricks, but despite his fatigue, he never lay down in a bed but only slept a few hours in a chair. He ruptured the veins in his legs from the long hours of constant standing, and he would have to wrap them in gauze. He wore chains on his body, and they opened wounds on his back.

At that time, the monastery of Zographou on the Holy Mountain did not have enough monks to sustain it, so the Holy Synod of the Church of Bulgaria decided to send some monks from Bulgaria to make up the numbers. When they asked Father Evthymius if he would like to go, he accepted with great joy, and on October 21, 1969, he and Father John, a monk from the same monastery, made the journey to Zographou.

The abbot of Zographou at the time was Father Dometius, a Romanian from the cell of Saint Hypatius, which belonged to the monastery of Vatopedi. He had agreed to take on the abbacy temporarily, though without leaving his cell, until a Bulgarian was found, and then to hand over the abbacy to him. Upon his arrival, Father Evthymius immediately gained the trust of the fathers of Zographou on account of his virtues, and in 1971 they elected him to the office of *proistamenos*. Four years later, on the eleventh of November 1975, they unanimously elected him abbot. On account of his great humility he did not want the abbacy and held firm on his rejection, though the fathers insisted. It was not until the Virgin Mary appeared to him and said, "You must accept; there is no one else," that he relented and by the Panagia's command became abbot, a position he kept for the next twenty-five years. He never lost his simplicity and humility, however. He never showed off, or even behaved like the head of a monastery, but rather preferred to operate away from the spotlight. He was always the first to help with any work that needed to be done, and he sacrificed himself for his monastery.

Apart from the responsibilities of the abbot, he also took on the job of secretary, reading and answering letters. He had picked up a bit of Greek in Bulgaria, but during his time at Zographou he cultivated it to the point where he could read and write in Katharevousa[3] and converse with Greek pilgrims and state employees.

He also took on the job of steward, traveling to Thessaloniki on his own to shop for the needs of the monastery. He always went to the market with an old, light blue bag, never using a taxi but carrying the shopping by hand back to the *konaki*.[4] When he was finished with the business and provisions, he would take the bus to Halkidiki and from there take everything to the monastery.

During his time in Thessaloniki he lived simply and ascetically. He never forgot the services. He did all of them with a prayer-rope, a psalter, and a prayer book, as he did not have all the necessary service books. When it was time for a service, he would shut himself in his room and pray. He did many prostrations and so many times could not hear the door. He did not lock it, however, so that if someone needed to come in and ask a question, he would answer as necessary and then continue his prayer.

Every morning he would do the full service of Matins, and many times the vestryman, who stayed with him, would become impatient with the delay, as they had many tasks to complete. He would repeatedly knock on the door to get the elder to speed up so that they could get to their errands, but the elder would not rush. He always prioritized his spiritual responsibilities, finishing them first, and only then they would begin with their worldly work, many times without eating breakfast. When they returned to the *konaki* in the evening, exhausted, the elder would begin to cook some vegetables, but the vestryman was hungry and would always eat some bread or fruit. The elder patiently waited, eating only at the appointed time. He never ate outside the appointed monastic mealtimes, whether at the monastery or elsewhere.

---

3   A high, "pure" form of Greek developed after the Turkish occupation in an attempt to return to the complexity of the Attic dialect, which had been the official and literary language of the later Roman Empire . —ED.

4   A house for monastics to lodge when away from their monastery.—TRANS.

He never went to restaurants, saying that it is not appropriate for a monastic. Once, the vestryman insisted they go out, and in obedience the elder went to the restaurant, but during the whole meal one could see that he was sorrowful. When there was no food at the *konaki*, he would crack a few walnuts and get through the night that way.

Once, he withdrew about a million drachmas[5] from the bank for the monastery's needs. In 1986, that was quite a bit of money, and it seems that someone was watching him, because as soon as he came out, someone sped by on a motorcycle, snatching his tattered blue bag, in which he had put the money, and quickly disappearing. The elder only managed to call out, "Wait, why are you taking it? That is monastic money!"

That night he told the vestryman what had happened, but recounted it calmly, without sorrow. Afterwards, he went to bed as normal, as if nothing had happened, falling asleep quickly. He had probably prayed quite a bit for the thief.

When he was outside Athos, in the city, he did not immerse himself in what was going on around him. He was careful, which is why he was able to preserve his spiritual state intact. And when he returned to the monastery, he would immediately resume being the celebrant at the daily services, as there were very few priests. Travelworn as he was, he would put on his stole and begin Vespers. The next day during Divine Liturgy, while reading the Gospel, his voice would be altered by compunction and his eyes would fill with tears. Going out into the world did not alter him, as he was watchful and he only went out when necessary. "He who in actually going out does not go out."[6]

He would feel the same deep prayerfulness on Sunday nights, when he read the Salutations to Saint George. When he was not the celebrant, he sat in the chanter's stand, as he loved to read and chant. He read the Psalter, the canons, and the hours, slowly and clearly, without rushing. When there was no one else chanting, he did both chanters' parts himself, without complaint. He neither reprimanded

---

5   Approximately $3500-$4000. One must keep in mind that at the time things in Greece cost very little, and a single drachma could buy quite a bit. —TRANS.
6   *The Ladder of Divine Ascent* 27:5.

nor condemned the other monks for their absence but was always peaceful and quiet.

Since at the time the monks at Zographou were from different monasteries in Bulgaria, they did not keep a strict coenobitic order. The elder did not intervene in the monks' personal lives unless they asked him to do so but always treated them with maternal love. There were two things, however, about which he was unyielding: he did not allow talking in church, and if two monks had argued, he insisted they be reconciled before Matins.

He also insisted that the services be celebrated with order and piety, without abbreviations. Once, the monk responsible for the Typikon[7] made a mistake and they skipped a canon to the Theotokos. After the service, the elder called a monk to come with him and they read it by themselves in the chapel of the Virgin Mary. Even though he was tired, he combated his sleepiness and they read the canon.

How could the elder not be tired when he was constantly running to do any work that was needed and slept very little or, on certain nights, not at all? Very often he would return from Thessaloniki, take over as daily celebrant, celebrate Vespers, and afterwards knead and make the next day's prosphora until late at night. Then he would prepare to serve liturgy and immediately go to the church, without so much as an hour's rest. It was natural for him to be exhausted with so much work and no sleep. Once, while moving hay with a tractor, he fell asleep at the wheel and drove the tractor into the river. The Panagia then appeared to him again and saved him, so that he came out without a scratch. She then said to him, "Stop with the ascetic excesses! Had I not come, do you know what would have happened to you?"

Another time, after Compline, he went to a cell named 'Patiteria' [Wine-presses], where they produced the raki, and spent the night with the workers. The abbot had humbly asked the vestryman [ἐπίτροπος] if a monk could stay with them, but the vestryman judged that it was better for the abbot to go, so that the workers would not misappropriate the raki. Around 3am they finished the work, and the abbot

---

7   Rubric for how to execute the services.—TRANS.

took the raki to the underground storage. He then immediately put on his cassock and cowl and went to church. The sacristan saw all this when he went to strike the talanton.[8] Seeing him sleepy during the service, one of the monks criticized the abbot; the abbot, who heard him, did not say anything, but the sacristan immediately spoke up, and they all marveled at the elder's humility and self-denial.

There was another time when he was up all night looking for certain documents in the archives. Without any sleep, he went to Simonopetra the next morning in order to photocopy them. While there, they asked him to serve in the Divine Liturgy, and without any sleep, he prepared and served. He celebrated simply, humbly, and with emotion. He was an excellent celebrant, knowing many of the prayers by heart.

He showed love to everyone, no matter what their ethnicity or social position. All who met him witnessed his humility and his love, from the policemen serving at the guardhouse to the Areopagites from Athens.[9]

Kyriakos Keskesiadie who served as policeman at Zographou for many years would say, "The elder never denied the policeman and workers any hospitality and help he could offer. We were friends, and many times I would go to the abbot's quarters to talk. Many times, while we were speaking, he would get sleepy from his fatigue. He went and did all the work. He did not have any helpers. He always had a smile and never got angry. Once, I had gone out to hunt and was in the river in some bushes. When it got dark, I heard something approaching, making noise and breaking branches. It was not a boar, as boars would have sniffed me out, so I shone my flashlight at it, yelled, and heard something going up onto the road. I thought that it might be a thief, so I ran after him. Finally I saw the elder, who was trying to get into a car. I asked him:

"'Why didn't you answer?'

"'I was afraid; I didn't know who it was.'

"'What were you looking for down there?'

8   Specially carved, wooden board struck with a wooden mallet to call monks to the church for prayers.—TRANS.

9   Judges of the Areopagus, that is, the Supreme Court of Greece.—ED.

"'A herb I want to put inside the wine barrels. I know it grows down there.'"

George Sidiropoulos, the customs officer, mentioned the following: "I served on the Holy Mountain since 1977, and from 1987-1992 I served at Zographou. Before my tenure there, I would visit the monastery on pilgrimage and to see the elder. I knew him as a true monk, a man of prayer. He was the abbot, but he looked like an ascetic, an anchorite. He loved everyone, the fathers, the pilgrims and the workers alike. Many times he served us in the dining hall and the guest quarters by himself. He always seemed tired but never refused to receive someone for confession or conversation. He had a lot of patience and kindness, and he never complained. When I went to serve at Zographou, the building which housed the customs office was in a horrible condition. The elder took interest and encouraged me to be patient,while at the same time sending workers to make the necessary repairs. I saw him working everywhere, in the church, the guesthouse, the refectory, the garden… When necessary, he also served as chauffer, driving pilgrims or monks to-and-fro. Once, the feast of the monastery was drawing near and we were discussing how we could get enough fish. I offered to go and buy some, but he suggested that we throw a net into the sea. We caught eighty kilos of fish, which sufficed for the feast.

"One winter it had snowed heavily and there was over a meter of snow on the ground. The pilgrims were trapped and worried. The elder said, 'We'll open the footpath,' and began working first; the others then followed, and the footpath was opened.

"When I visited him in the abbot's quarters, I saw that when he wanted to rest he did not lie down but rather sat in a chair. I asked him the reason, to which he replied, 'a monk must always be ready, alert, watchful, because he does not know when the Lord will call him, either on this earth, for some task, or in the next, to be close to Him.' The elder recommended that I also rest in a chair, so I tried to imitate him.

"The elder was not comfortable when there was much heat during the winter. He would say, 'Heat relaxes us, and easy living is not fitting for a monk.'

"He helped me understand the meaning of life. He counseled me, 'Love your neighbor as yourself.' The elder taught me to try to do the best I could for others. I learned the basic virtues from him: love for God and for your fellow man.

"I would feel joy being with him. Every so often he would do me the honor of coming to the customs office and speaking with me. He was very humble.

"When the visitors saw him, they would tell me, 'This monk must be very pious and hardworking,' and when I would tell them he was the abbot, they rejoiced even more.

"When I caught a few fish, I would give some to the elder when he came to see me at the customs office. He did not want to take anything and only took half of a small fish so that I wouldn't be saddened.

"I was not afraid, living alone at the customs office by the port, because I would say, 'I have Saint George who protects me and the elder who prays for me.' To this day I feel great joy every time I remember him."

A certain Athonite hierodeacon expressed his desire never to leave Mount Athos for any reason and prayed to the Panagia to grant him this wish. When the elder learned of it, he said, 'This is the first thing a good monk should ask from the Panagia. Whenever a monk goes out into the world, he loses some of his wages.'

The biological father of Father Mark from Konstamonitou was at the port one day, when, for an unknown reason, a layman from Halkidiki began to curse Elder Evthymius with foul words. The humble elder lowered his head and did not say anything. Where the layman stood there was an old stone bridge, and a week later the same layman was standing in the same place below the bridge. Suddenly, without any obvious reason, the bridge collapsed on top of him and the man died beneath the stones.

Here is the testimony of an Athonite: "Elder Evthymius was modest, serious, and at the same time sweet, joyful, and hardworking. He loved the services, and was filled with the fear of God and a deep sense of his monastic character and his duty to the monastery.

"Even though he was amiable, he always inspired respect and reserve, as he was a spiritual monk whose concern was unceasing prayer. You felt that he was living great spiritual experiences. He lived like a simple monk and did not enjoy the honors of his office as abbot. He lived with a constant underlying concern for the monastery, which suffered from lack of monks and severe building issues. He managed, however, to keep the monastery intact despite all the difficulties because he had faith in God, love for Saint George, and care for both the material and the spiritual."

There were several times when a certain bad-tempered monk behaved insultingly towards him, calling him a "carcass," but the elder did not respond at all. Later, this same monk was attacked by many temptations and finally he left the monastery completely. He had served as bursar, and when he handed over the office, there were funds missing. Some suggested taking him to court, but the all-forgiving elder took his side. 'It is not right,' he would say. 'We are monks.'

Abbot Evthymius was a pious man who loved prayer and had hidden inner spiritual works. He was always saying the Jesus prayer and reading the works of the Watchful Fathers, particularly Saint Isaac the Syrian and the Life and Work of Saint Païsius Velichovsky. He would tell prospective monks that a book is like a mirror, because within it you see yourself, your spiritual state.

He never missed a service. Despite his many obligations, he always found the time to fulfill his spiritual responsibilities.

Once, he fell from a persimmon tree and had to go to the hospital for treatment. He did not leave off his spiritual obligations, even there, and would try to finish his daily prayers before the other patients in his ward woke up. One day he was sitting on his bed saying the Jesus prayer rather hurriedly, when the Panagia appeared to him for a third time. He saw her clearly, though from piety and respect he did not dare to lift his eyes to look at her again. He heard her tell him that he should not rush when he is praying. He was forced to recount this event to a certain hieromonk, who is now a Metropolitan in Bulgaria, because at one point they were doing a service in the *konaki* in Thessaloniki and the then hieromonk was reading quickly in order to have time for the daily work.

Elder Evthymius loved all-night vigils and participated in them with joy. He chanted very sweetly and reverently, even though he was not musically trained. Often, when he chanted a troparion, he was choked by compunction and unable to finish.

He was a true hesychast, even though he never stopped working. A certain monk suggested that they leave the monastery and go become hesychasts at the port. The elder, who lived the hesychastic life in his heart, did not accept, even though he desired it, saying, "Silence is good, but I cannot leave the monastery."

He was a true abbot and wholly fulfilled the saying, 'and he that is chief, let him be as he that doth serve' (Lk. 22:26). He did any and all jobs as though he were the least of the workers. After the service he would wear an old short cassock and go clean the road towards the water pumps or fix damage to the pipes. Once, when there was a serious problem with the water pipes, many men went to help, but as the work dragged on with no end in sight, they got tired and left, until at last only the elder and the vestryman remained. They kept digging, and finally found the problem. And even though it was nighttime, the elder masterfully reconnected the pipes, returning to the monastery at 1am. That same piping works to this very day.

He fixed the roofs, gathered walnuts and other fruit, and climbed up trees until his death. He was baker and prosphoro-maker. He made wine and produced raki at night, on his own or with another lay worker. He helped Mitsos the cook haul warm water, so as not to bother the other monks.

When a certain monk came from Bulgaria to live at Zographou, the elder took the mules down to the port to wait for him so that he would not have to walk to the monastery alone. He received him with heartfelt love, embracing him and kissing his hand. They went to Karyes to get his papers in order, and while at the *konaki*, the elder gathered white beans and laid a table for him.

Despite all this, some criticized him for not restorating any buildings at the monastery. But the situation was difficult at that time, and even though he wished it, he could not do much since the monastery lacked both manpower and funds. He tried to help the monastery, but his heart was not attached to material things. When a young monk showed him some plans for expanding and restoring the monastery, he told him, "These things (construction, et cetera.) are good, but we should not get excessively caught up in them."

He was ascetic. Even though he tired out his body, he ate little. He wanted food to be cooked simply. When the vestryman suggested that they put more things on the table, the elder replied, "It is not necessary. We have enough. We are monks. We should eat a few simple things." But he always insisted that there be enough bread for everyone. If they forgot to set out food for him, he would not comment or ask for it. He only ate at the refectory. If they offered him something to eat, even something small, after Compline, he refused.

He never judged anyone and a foul word never came out of his mouth. He had a nobility and a sensitivity and never spoke scornfully towards anyone.

All the monks at Zographou had been to Jerusalem at least once, but the elder had never gone. In the last year of his life, he told someone, "Every Divine Liturgy is like going to Jerusalem."

He loved all equally: Bulgarians, Greeks, Russians, and whoever else met him testified to this. He loved his fatherland fervently but in a spiritual way, without nationalism. During the time that atheist communism reigned in Bulgaria, the elder published spiritual books and on his own initiative sent them to Bulgaria to support the faithful. Even though the monastery did not have much income, he spent three and a half million drachmas[10] towards that purpose.

He was completely possessionless. For a time, the Synod of the Church of Bulgaria sent a small amount of financial assistance to every Bulgarian monk. The elder never touched this money but put it aside and later told the vestryman to take it and put it in the church.

He always wore old clothing. Once, he bought a warm vest for the winter, but another monk asked why he did not buy one for him also. The very next day the elder gave him the vest and put on his own old, tattered vest again. He washed his clothes by hand in cold water, even in the winter.

---

10 $12,250–$13,000.—TRANS.

He adored and was utterly devoted to the Panagia. He would often repeat, with compunction, the story of her climbing the stairs of the temple on her own when she was three years old.

Even though he was greatly talented and knowledgeable, he never boasted; quite the opposite. When he did some job, he would always ask someone else for advice, in order not to have the job done only according to the way he himself desired. In the Synaxis of Elders he would express his opinion, but he did not try to enforce it. He quietly prayed, and after the discussions, what he wanted would always happen.

For ascetic reasons he rarely lit a fire in his room. Every so often, when it was late and he wanted some warmth, he would go into the kitchen and sit next to the stove. But as he was always sleep-deprived, he would immediately fall asleep. Out of reverence, Mitsos the cook would stand next to him to protect him from falling off of his chair. But even he would get tired and fall sleep standing up.

He never lay down in a bed to rest but sat in a chair or a couch. He wanted to be ever vigilant, like a soldier, and it was there, sitting on a couch, that the fathers found him on the twenty-first of November 1994, after the vigil of the Entrance of the Theotokos into the temple. His pure soul had flown to heaven to be near Christ, whom he had loved from his youth and served in every way throughout his life.

The fathers observed that on his bed lay a thick layer of dust and cobwebs.

In this life, Elder Evthymius never enjoyed sleep or rest, but now may the Lord, the righteous judge, grant him rest in His ageless blessedness.

All who knew him remember him with love as a holy man.

May we have his blessing. Amen.

Elder Metrophanes of Saint Paul's

Elder Metrophanes of Saint Paul's

Elder Metrophanes was formerly married. He was born on February 21, 1917, in the village of Korthion on the island of Andros. His parents, John and Helen Konti, baptized him and named him George. He became a non-commissioned officer in the Royal Hellenic Navy and got married, but soon thereafter his wife got sick and they had to amputate her legs. He served her for about six to twelve months, after which she died. He had read Saint Paul and Saint Kosmas Aitolos and took their words to heart when they said that it is better for a widower not to remarry but rather become a monk. He had no children or obligations, so at the age of forty-five he left the world and came to the Holy Mountain. He gave away all his possessions to the poor, taking only twenty thousand drachmas with him. He went all around the Holy Mountain visiting all the monasteries twice, after which he decided to stay at Saint Paul's. When he went to do the customary prostration asking to be a novice, he told the Synaxis of the monastery, "I visited all the monasteries, but I found inner peace here." He gave the twenty thousand drachmas to the elder, who asked him, "Do you not have relatives?" George replied, "They have already had their share; this is for the souls of my parents." He became a monk on January 30, 1965, with the name Metrophanes.

His previous life is almost completely unknown, as he never mentioned it. He became a monk and lived an impeccable life, with hidden spiritual works. He was the model of detachment, obedience, neptic occupation and monastic exactness.

He never went out into the world, except for one time, a year before his death, to visit a doctor. He had no communication with his relatives, reaching the heights of worldly detachment. At one point his brother came to the monastery and the elder greeted him and then left. His brother ran after him to speak to him, but Elder Metrophanes just kept working. As he was leaving, the brother took out twenty thousand drachmas to give to the elder, which in 1970 was a lot of money. The elder did not take it, responding, "My monastery has everything it needs." His brother did not come again, though his nephews visited him. He greeted them in the courtyard but did not speak to them again.

As he had not taken the money, they sent him a check. He took it to the abbot sorrowfully, saying, "*Geronda*, forgive me. They are putting me into temptation. Take the money for the needs of the monastery, otherwise I will send it back."

He served in the guesthouse for about twenty years, which was a meeting place. There were people that came to Saint Paul's just to see him, as they knew that he did not speak. They sent him greeting cards, which he did not open. Some people would ask him:

"Father Metrophanes, do you remember us? We were here last year." And in order to avoid discussion he would say:

"Blessed child, they'll be ringing soon. They'll be ringing the bells for church."

"You don't remember us? From the Theological School..."

"The elder says we must always be at Vespers from the very beginning."

When he wanted to avoid pointless questions, he would say, "I don't know, go ask the elder."

When someone asked him where he was from, he would avoid the question saying, "Lord Jesus Christ, have mercy on me." If the other insisted, saying, "I asked you where you are from!" he would say, "Please!" and then repeat, a little louder, "Lord Jesus Christ have mercy on me." They would ask him, "Elder, when did you come to the monastery?" to which he would reply, "The abbot knows." He avoided conversation, especially with lay people, but despite that the pilgrims weren't upset or saddened by his refusal; on the contrary, they would afterwards send letters saying, "Congratulations on your guestmaster!"

And indeed, he was worthy of congratulations, because as much as he avoided conversation with the visitors, so much was he detailed in his job and did everything in his power to make sure that they were comfortable. The visitors felt his love. As guestmaster he had many large tubs for washing the sheets, which he had for many years. He washed them all by hand, and his hands would bleed from the detergent and cleaning products. He never gave anyone reason to criticize him for neglect. He was quiet, extremely polite, and spoke to everyone in the plural number.[1] He also had the gift of not judging.

He was a man of prayer and in the beginning had a hard time with the service of guestmaster, because every so often he would have to miss a service, which he did not want to do. He sought advice from Father Ephraim in Katounakia, who told him, "Obedience first, even if you miss out a bit on service and prayer." After this he was at peace and did his job heartily, without any more troubling thoughts.

He always considered obedience first and foremost. He often read the book of Saints Barsanuphius and John and held it second only to the Gospels.

He was a pillar of obedience. They once gave him the task of taking caring of an ill-tempered, disabled old elder, who gave him a very hard time. When the old monk did not like the food, he would throw it on the ground and do other such things. Elder Metrophanes confessed his difficulties to his elder, and continued his service with forbearance. The old monk softened up in the end, even asking for forgiveness and thanking him for everything.

All his fellow monks witness that he was at a very high spiritual level. He had nobility and sensitivity and was very attentive to his thoughts. He confessed and repented for bad thoughts as though he had committed a crime. He did not burden anyone, he had no demands, and he was obedient to everyone. When, on January 1, everyone would receive his new obediences, he would go in, do a

---

1   Addressing an individual with the second person plural form of the pronoun and verb is a sign of deferrence in several languages, including Russian, French, and German. This also was the case in Early Modern English, where 'ye/you' was the second person plural personal pronoun used in this way, as opposed to 'thou/thee' which was the informal or familiar second person singular. —ED.

prostration, and regardless of what they gave him, he would say, 'May it be blessed.' He said nothing else, neither complaining, nor arguing, nor saying that he is unable. He was always peaceful, silent, and neptic. He had an internal spiritual occupation and ceaseless prayer. In his cell he had a seat that fit him and he would stay up at night saying the Jesus prayer. He had also placed two pieces of wood to fit his head, so that he slept sitting down. During services he stood and prayed on his prayer-rope. He forced himself[2] to stand, so that sleep would not overtake him. The fatigue from his vigils was evident, as sometimes, even though he was standing, his prayer-rope would fall to the ground. He was extremely tall and suffered pain in his lower back.

Elder Metrophanes was a man of prayer, and he safeguarded noetic prayer as the apple of his eye. He never sat down for idle chat, nor did he ever speak about spiritual matters, even with the fathers. He would only speak generally, saying things like, "Spring came early this year," or "It rained today." A couple words, and then he would discreetly depart; he would go be on his own and pray on the prayer-rope.

In jobs requiring all hands, he helped silently, without stopping the Jesus prayer. If he heard young monks idly chatting, he would say, indefinitely and in a general way, without looking at anyone, "The prayer, fathers, the prayer." Other times, when the young monks forgot and were not saying the prayer, he would discerningly say the Jesus prayer once out loud as a reminder. He would ask Father Anthimos: "How are you doing with the prayer, father? Are you working on the prayer?"

"Yes, Elder. I am saying my prayer rule, I am trying."

"Blessed man, the prayer rule is one thing, the Jesus prayer another."

Once, a young monk living next to him asked him about the Jesus prayer, to which he replied, "I do not know about such things."

The young monk mentioned this to the abbot, and the abbot told him to tell Elder Metrophanes that he had the abbot's blessing to tell

---

2   Or "he exercised violence on himself (Gr. βίαζε); see Mt. 11:12.—ED.

him. When the young monk then told the elder, the elder spoke to him, telling him about circular prayer as he himself understood it and practiced it. He told him that during the service he listened to the chanting here and there, but his main focus was on the prayer. Generally he would say the Jesus prayer unceasingly all day and night, even in his sleep, except at the refectory, where he could not, a fact which caused him great sadness and pain: "How's this?" he would say.

We do not know if someone had taught him the Jesus prayer, but he was a very disciplined individual and he latched on to whatever spiritually benefited him with great zeal, avoiding whatever did the opposite. And so, with his persistence in the prayer, God taught him noetic prayer and he was able to 'pray ceaselessly.'

He was very humble. Someone once asked him:

"Why don't you go practice hesychasm, since you like the Jesus prayer?" to which he replied, "Such things are for the strong, not for me."

And yet, Elder Metrophanes achieved a great feat: to live hesychastically in a coenobium. A hesychast is not one who lives in the desert, but one who does the work of hesychasm. "A hesychast is he who strives to confine his incorporeal being within his bodily house, paradoxical as this is" (*The Ladder*, 27:6). The one who is silent and the one who prays noetically and unceasingly is a hesychast. This is hesychasm, constant retention of prayer, and Elder Metrophanes achieved this remarkable noetic feat, all while living in a busy monastery.

A military academy cadet who visited Saint Paul's told us the following: "I got up in the middle of the night to go to the bathroom, and in the corridor across the way, a way off, I saw Elder Metrophanes and he seemed to be whispering. That very moment I perceived a sweet smell emanating from his mouth and spreading through the whole corridor, and I was filled with peace and calm. Elder Metrophanes turned and went up the stairs and I went to the restroom, but that fragrance and inner peace and calm remained, even in the bathroom. The whole corridor had been suffused with that sweet smell."

Once, the tempter tempted him, telling him that he had not done a pure confession and he would go to hell. Elder Metrophanes then sat down and in a notebook wrote out a detailed and complete confession going back to his childhood. He went to the abbot and read the document, a task which took over two hours. When he was finished, he crossed himself and said, "Glory to Thee, O God! I thank thee, Lord! Elder, my soul has been refreshed. Now I will be able to respond to the tempter and tell him that I confessed everything in detail."

The devil, however, did not remain quiet. He moved from an inward war, with temptations, to an outward one. When Elder Metrophanes was sleeping, he would go underneath the bed and start shaking it and making noise, not letting the elder sleep.

He often saw the devil, clear as day. His cell would fill with demons, one sitting on the shelf, another beneath the bed, all naked. He mentioned it to the elder: "Who are they, Elder? Outside it is snowing, and they are completely naked. Don't they get cold? They won't leave me in peace."

Even when he had gone out to the hospital for his health, the devil bothered him. One day the doctors got worried because the night before he had suddenly sat up wide eyed, staring into the darkness. It was obvious that he was somehow struggling internally, and the doctors and nurses surrounded him, but they could not bring him back. This lasted for two hours and then he came back to himself. When they asked him what had happened, he laughed and simply said, "It was the unwanted one."

He wore clean but old cassocks, with a lot of patches. He did not intend to change out of his cassock, which he had worn consistently for the last twenty-four years, until they called him to the Synaxis and the abbot told him to wear a new one. He immediately said 'May it be blessed,' and obeyed. His stockings were so patched up that the original stocking was no longer visible. He was happy with simple, monastic things, and he respected the tradition of the elder monks. When he was in charge of the refectory, a younger monk who was working with him found a table with wheels and took it into the refectory to make their serving easier. As soon as Elder Metrophanes saw it, he yelled: "No, no, no! We shall do things the way we were taught," and so they did not use it. He had learned the way things were done in the monastery, and he loved and kept that order with piety and consistency.

He never had any demands. He once needed to have some medical exams, so he told the monastery doctor and then waited patiently, saying, "If they want, they'll take me."

He went out to Thessaloniki to have surgery for hernia, and he needed to be transferred to another hospital for a checkup. He would not let Father Sophrony take his bag, however much he pleaded with him.

Dr. Panagiotis Koliomichalis narrated the following: "In the 1980s I was struggling with many temptations and had arrived at despair. I went to the Holy Mountain to find someone to help me. I traveled with a silent, unknown monk who was uncharacteristically tall. At one point, the silent monk turned and asked me:

"'What's the matter? It seems that something is troubling you deeply.'

"I told him my problem and asked for his advice. He considered for a while, and then said, 'You should watch for three things. The first is patience.'

"I rejoiced inwardly, as I was patient by nature, so I already possessed one of the three things that would help me. I then eagerly awaited the other two. The elder continued:

"'If your initial patience cracks, you must gather courage and be patient again.'

"'Good,' I thought inwardly. This seems achievable too. I then asked:

"'And the third, Elder?'

"'You must have patience.'

"I was overcome with joyful sadness. Joy, because I knew what I had to do, and sadness because it was not something that would miraculously help me.

"When we arrived at the monastery, I realized that he was the guestmaster. He gave me twice the normal welcome treats, saying with love, 'Take these also, as you are tired and troubled.'

"Other pilgrims told me that his name was Metrophanes, and when I told this story to others, everyone had a hard time believing it, knowing how quiet and laconic he was. His counsel helped me and I thank him for his prayers."

He served until his old age, serving as monastery pharmacist in the last years of his life until his death.

In the end, he suffered from heart disease. Father Anthimos went to see him at the hospital, and he prayed for him and made the sign of the cross over him. He then asked the administrator if they had any issues or complaints with the patient, and he answered, "You did not send us a man; you sent us an angel." They said the same thing to the abbot.

After he returned to the monastery, during the last week of his life, his disease had progressed, and it was with difficulty that he went down for the Divine Liturgy.

On the last day of his life, half an hour before falling asleep in the Lord wearing the cassock in which he was tonsured a monk, he went down into the courtyard and walked around the monastery, as if he wanted to bid farewell to the places where he had lived and struggled for so many years, and afterwards he went back up to his cell. He saw someone whitewashing the next cell over and said, "How beautiful, what a clean white cell. That's the way it should be. It will be a great joy for the one who lives there." He sat in the seat where he kept vigil with the prayer-rope, and as he was saying the Jesus prayer, he peacefully fell asleep in the Lord. They buried him with the shoes and cassock he was wearing, as those were part of his monasticism.

A little while after he passed, the monk in charge of serving him brought up his food and seeing him in this position thought he was praying. Not wanting to wake him up, he put down the tray and left. After half an hour he came back to take it and found it untouched, so he gently nudged him, and immediately understood that he had departed. It was April 28, 1995, at 8 in the morning, and Elder Metrophanes had been seventy-eight years old. As with all the fathers, he did not go through rigor mortis, and his body was as soft and pliable as if he was alive. He was sitting in his chair, his head bent to the right, holding his prayer-rope, with his nail on the knot. The fathers present saw his face shining, and they felt such reverence that they hesitated even to touch him in order to prepare him for burial. No one had any complaint of Elder Metrophanes. On the contrary, they held him as an example of a perfect monk. Not only did he have no spiritual debts, but he had done seventy-five canons of prayer for his soul.

Eusebius, the former abbot that had tonsured him a monk, admiringly described his monastic way of life and virtue in glowing terms.

The current abbot also bears witness: "In all my life I have never seen a monk more prudent than Father Metrophanes. He was a monastic paradigm. And he achieved this because he never judged anyone. He had true nobility."

One of the fathers saw him in his dreams twice and asked him how he was. "Glory be to God, I am very well." Seeing him wearing the schema, he said, "I see that you are wearing a schema," to which the elder replied "Well, of course I am wearing it, because it is with this that I fought the good fight."

May we have his blessing. Amen.

Elder George of Saint Paul's Monastery

Father George was born Gerasimus Moschonas on September 6, 1910, in the village of Havdata on Kephalonia. His father died from appendicitis at the age of thirty-five, and this was the first time the child thought about monasticism. "When I saw my father dead, I said, it's over. There is nothing better than monasticism."

His father's brother Kyriakos protected the orphans and worked hard to make sure they had a financially secure future. Fifteen years later, in 1929, the uncle went to the Holy Mountain and was tonsured a monk with the name Constantine. He had made a vow many years earlier to do so, as his life had been saved during the war.

The young Gerasimus worked in Athens and in Piraeus and helped his siblings as much as he could, particularly Anthony. He would say, "If I had stayed in the world, I would have become Croesus. I was working and the money was flowing."

In 1935, after he finished his time in the army, he came to the Holy Mountain to visit his uncle, out of gratitude. Even though he was a lively youth, he was inspired by the life of the fathers and his uncle, and decided to stay and become a monk.

After a period of novitiate, he was tonsured on December 20, 1937, and received the name George. He struggled willingly and was very attentive to his work and services. He was successful in everything. He was the best cook of the monastery and also the best gardener; his garden could have been in an exhibit. When the fathers went to the nightly service, he would dig deep in the garden, nearly a meter down, with his two-prong hoe, while saying the prayer. His tomato plants became so tall that he needed a ladder to gather all the tomatoes. He was also the best baker. He would knead and say, "I will make such bread, that you will want to have bread with your bread." It was, indeed, delicious. He was also an excellent fisherman. Whatever he did turned out exceptional and superior, and he did it with his heart, in order to bring joy to the fathers.

At that time, they would invite chanters for the vigils and pay them, as no one in the monastery knew how to chant. Father George could not tolerate this, so he went to New Skete, learned music under a certain Father Hesychius, and then came back and taught Abbot Parthenius and other fathers, so the monastery then had chanters. His voice was not so great, but he knew the music well and would say jokingly, "Alright, I know I'm not arch-chanter material, but I'm too good to be a second!" He helped the monastery a great deal, with work, in administration, and also as representative and chairman.

During the German occupation he was gardener and they initiated him into the Resistance. Along with other monks, he would help resistance fighters escape to the East. He was betrayed by a Romanian, and the Germans arrested him and led him to the army base "Pavlos Melas," where he underwent a military trial. The judge asked him:

"Why are you taking the enemy and sending them to Smyrna and Egypt?"

"Because they are in need," he answered. "If someone knocks on your door, what do you do? In the Gospel, Christ says to help those in need."

The judge then asked, "So if a German came and asked you for help, you would help him?"

"If he needs help, of course. Depending on what his needs are. But you do not have any needs. You've drowned the world in blood. You have made the blood of humanity flow."

The court condemned him to death, and they took him to the prison at the Heptapyrgion.[1] Two days later, he contracted malaria and got sick. They took him to the medical ward, where two monks, who were also biological brothers, Panteleimon and Theophylact Nanopoulos from the cell of the Copyists (*Typographi*) in Karyes, and

---

1   A seven-towered fortress overlooking Thessaloniki.—ED.

Elder Meletius of Sykies were. Father George was burning with fever, but one night, just as it got dark, he came to, sat up on his bed and said: "Saint Paul just came to me with Saint George and told me that they will free me in three days." The others did not believe him, thinking he was speaking in a feverish delirium—and, indeed, Father George fell into a lethargic sleep. At 3pm three days later, however, though he could not stand on his feet from the fever and exhaustion, he jumped out of the third floor onto a tree and escaped without as much as a scratch. Though the place was strictly guarded, no one noticed him.

He started for the monastery, knowing that only there would he be safe, as anywhere outside there was danger of being re-apprehended. He began on foot, without knowing in which direction he was going, and arrived at Gomati, where an informant of the Germans saw him and said, "You are suspicious! You're under arrest." He took out a revolver, and threatening him, he made Father George walk ahead of him. At one point, Father George pretended that he had stumbled on the path, and swinging around quickly, he took the pistol. The man then began to beg for his life, saying, "Spare me, I have a wife and children." He did, indeed, spare him, and he continued to the Holy Mountain, but he held onto the 'iron', which is what he called the revolver. At Monoxyliti, at the Dionysian place, he was in danger of being recognized by a worker from the neighboring village, but he kept his wits and managed to escape and reach the monastery. He did not go inside, however, but remained in a cave above the monastery, and only abbot Seraphim, Father Andrew (who was in charge of the refectory), and Father David knew that he was there. Father Andrew went and secretly communed him on Saturdays when he celebrated liturgy at the cemetery. The place where they met was another cave, the cave of Saint Paul, visible only from above the monastery's tower. He lived in that cave for nineteen months, and during that time he suffered through an exceedingly harsh winter. He managed through various ingenious methods. He only lit a fire to warm the cave at night, so that the smoke would not give him away, and they lowered food to him over the monastery walls at night in a wicker basket.

In the spring, since the sun did not shine into the cave until much later in the day, he would go and sit on a rock across the way. An adder bit him there once, but he called on the Apostle Paul and did not suffer anything.

One day on the path to Karyes which passed below his cave, he saw three Romanians, one of them being the one who had betrayed him. He had the revolver with him and could have sought vengeance, but he simply said, "Let them go on their merry way."

The Germans soon came and decided to burn down the monastery, since they suspected that they were hiding Moschonas (Father George). They got mixed up, however, and instead of going to Saint Paul's, they went to Dionysiou. They gave the monks one week to gather their things and leave, and then they would burn down the monastery. When they understood that they had made a mistake, they got up to leave, but the abbot Gabriel delayed them, secretly sending someone to inform Saint Paul's that the Germans were coming. Then the fathers understood the words of Father Sophrony the Russian, who on the previous day had told them that all the fathers should pray in their cells because a great evil is coming to the monastery. The fathers, counseled by Father Theodosius who was the secretary, wrote out and signed an apparent condemnation of Father George, noting their decision to hand him over themselves when they saw him. When the Germans came, they showed them the document, and through the foreseeing grace of Father Sophrony, the monastery was saved.

When the German occupation ended and the danger passed, Father George came back to the monastery and resumed his work. He would say, "I went through difficult times, but I have never before experienced such a delight of soul. It was a blessing from Sts. Paul and George who freed me."

One of the people whom Father George had helped escape and save was the son of a minister in New Zealand. As soon as the war was over, he came to thank him with a sack full of liras, calling Father George his savior. The monk answered:

"God saved us both."

"My father sends these with all his love."

"I do not need them; I left such things behind when I came here."

"Take them for the monastery."

"The monastery doesn't need New Zealand money."

The New Zealander was moved, and later the government of New Zealand sent him an honorary title, naming him a "great benefactor of the country."

England sent him a medal as well, and wanted to give him a pension with English gold pounds, but he sent them back, saying, "I did what I did for my country." Many others who were saved by Father George were grateful and wanted to repay him, but he did not accept anything, even through those difficult post-war years of poverty and misery.

He had written an extensive diary, describing all that he had passed through. If it were published, it would have sold out. But one day, after his prayer rule, he burned it, saying, "Such things are not proper for monks."

Even though he was not highly educated, he successfully took on many of the monastery's serious affairs. He went to the bank with a money order from the monastery and took out the necessary funds for some monastery business, though he did not have an identity card, asking "Why do you want an identity card? It's me." Another time he took liras from the bank, put them in an old dirty carrier bag, put an old undershirt on top, and brought them to the monastery. When the conductor insisted that he put his carrier bag with the luggage, Father George refused, saying, "All the ladies have their purses, and I, as a monk, have my carrier bag."

Once a year, the monastery would send him to buy wheat from Kallikrateia, but one year he could not find wheat there and had to go to Thessaly. He took the bus to Larissa, and after a while, a woman came and sat next to him. He was tempted to look to see who she was, but immediately he began to argue with the thought, saying, "Why should I look?"

"To know with whom you are traveling."

"No, I will not look at her. Anyway, the Gospel says that if you look at a woman with desire, you have already committed adultery in your heart."

"Come on, a quick glance won't kill you. Perhaps it is a relative of yours."

In the end, though they traveled together from Thessaloniki to Larissa, a journey of several hours, he did not turn to look at her. He neither greeted her nor spoke with her, and once they arrived, he waited for the woman to disembark, only then getting up himself, so that he would not see her. He went about his business, and God rewarded him. He felt an indescribable sensation. He would later say, "the joy that I experienced... If this is the way it is in Paradise, I do not want anything more. And it was not for just a moment. It lasted for days. I left Larrisa, returned to the monastery, and it was still in my soul. A gladness of soul."

Father George was gifted, with many talents and with strength of soul. He excelled in everything he did, and he especially stood out in the monastic arena, ascending spiritually. He was, of course, a great spiritual fighter, but he was also helped a great deal by the counsels of the virtuous abbot of the monastery of Grigoriou, Athanasius. He held his advice second only to the Gospel, and he kept his counsels to the letter.

The abbot had told him, "You will never write a letter to anyone. You are finished with the world." And indeed, obeying his words, he never wrote a single line to anyone. Since he was often at the port, many knew him and sent him letters and greeting cards. He did not open them but gave them to someone else, saying, "See what this is, and if you want, answer it."

Elder Athanasius also told him: "A monk must despise his bed!" apparently meaning that he should not cherish it. And Father George said that he kept this counsel to the letter.

Abbot Athanasius had also said: "You will never light a lamp. You will go to your cell early, go to sleep early, and get up early for your prayer rule and the service." His spiritual father only needed to say it once, and Father George followed that rule for the rest of his life, never lighting a lamp.

The abbot also told him never to put water on his body. He followed this also, going even further, and refusing to ever bathe again. He would say, "Back in my village I was a dolphin, and swam all the time, but from the time I came to the monastery I did not go back into the sea." He would also say, "I'm in a longstanding fight with the broom and the mop."

His feet were like those of a tortoise and had become scaly, and his head looked as if he had dipped it in charcoal powder, but his body was extremely clean, like cotton. He did not smell, but his careless and filthy appearance put people off. Father George was like a valuable diamond purposefully thrown into mud and dirt, and this is what he wanted. He did it for asceticism and humility, so that people would look down on him. He tried to appear unimportant so that they would not honor him, and for this he purposely never bathed. When they put in liquid hand soap in the kitchens, he asked, impressed, "What is this?" and pushed the button. As soon as they told him it was soap, he wiped his hands on his cassock and said with wonder and obvious sorrow, "Oh, oh, oh... Soap!"

He never wore new clothes. He would say, "I will not become a slave to clothing. Neither the cowl nor the tonsure make a monk but only the desire for heaven and a godly life." When he went outside into the world for the affairs of the monastery, he paid some attention to his appearance, in order not to scandalize anyone. When he was in the monastery, however, his clothes were so dirty they could not be touched. He never changed his undershirt. If the first one did not dissolve on his body, he did not wear another. He had a torn cassock, and he sewed it up with thick wire, which showed. When his pants fell apart and he needed a new pair, he went to the laundry and took the oldest pair. If it was too long, he cut the bottom with a pocket knife. He did the same thing when he needed shoes. He would take and wear them, showing them to whomever they belonged, and would say with his characteristic joy: "May God forgive the sins of the man who lost these shoes." And once, when Father Gerasimus asked him if he had taken his shoes, he pretended to be offended and said, "What, are you calling me a thief?"

Father George did this so that he would always wear old things, as it was easy for the fathers to find other, new clothing. His way was beautiful, pleasant, and belied a spiritual and monastic depth.

He made no effort for external things, nor for money. When he was at the port, he took care of a little old elder, and when the old monk passed away, Father George found that he had seventy liras. He did not keep a single one. He gave them all to the monastery.

A fellow monk once teased him, saying:

"Father George, my teacher always said that cleanliness is next to Godliness."

"Ah, such things are for the worldly, Father. Saint Isaac says otherwise," he would respond wittily.

He often read the *Philokalia* which he called the 'great pamphlet' because it was so concise, and Saint Isaac the Syrian. He always had these two books with him and he would often refer to Saint Isaac to support whatever he said with patristic words.

He once told a monk, "I had a girlfriend (the *Philokalia*), and every time I faced any difficulty, I consulted her. She never led me astray."

Though he had only completed elementary school, he knew entire chapters of the *Philokalia* by heart. He had read the book so many times that the pages had melted. He generally avoided giving counsel, saying, "They have Moses and the Prophets." When they asked counsel of him, he would answer, "How can I counsel you, Father? I do not see myself as worthy. Each person knows in what way he will achieve salvation." He spoke to everyone in the plural number, even down to the last novice. He had a wellspring of politeness, always saying 'if you please,' and justifying his politeness in a graceful way, saying, "I had two neighbors named Eugenia;[2] I cannot insult them."

He loved the services very much. He would go down to the Church before the service started,and leave after it was finished. He never sat but always stood. Father Athanasius had told him never to sit during the liturgy.

An old abbot with the gift of discernment saw demons jumping into the monastery from the castle after compline and would tell the fathers, "Quick, go to your cells, fathers, quick, to your cells." The vestryman, who was a young monk and had heard this story, was a little afraid at night as he went around the monastery to wake the fathers up for the prayer rule, but afterwards he would go to the Church to light the vigil lamps, and he always found father George there, sitting

2   Greek for 'politeness'.—TRANS.

in the narthex, praying on his prayer-rope. Father George's presence comforted him, and the young monk once he asked him why he comes so early. Father George then told him, "When I was a young monk, there were two or three times when I was late getting to the service. I would say, 'Let the midnight office finish; I am tired.' Then I saw Saint Paul in my sleep holding his staff, and he said, 'Get up and go to the service, or I will break my staff on your back. Beware.'"

Father George had great monastic exactness. After compline, he neither drank nor ate anything. He would venerate the icons last, saying, "I know my place. I go last in order to be first." Naturally, he did not believe he would be first, but in this way he concealed his humility. He had so much piety that when he took antidoron or chrism during vigils, he did not turn his back to the priest, but left walking backwards.

He was counted worthy to see Saint Nectarius in a vision during a service: "I saw a bishop with all the episcopal vestments come out of the Great Doors. I was perplexed as to who it was, but my inner voice said, 'Saint Nectarius!' I ran and prostrated myself before him asking for his blessing: 'Grant me your blessing and pray for me me. Here at the monastery we do a vigil for you.' He made the sign of the cross over me, and after that everything disappeared."

Another time he said: "Once, while I was standing in the narthex and the fathers were coming out of the church, I saw something strange. Some fathers were dressed with all the monastic clothing, cassock, *skoupho*, cowl, schema, et cetera. But there were some that were missing the cowl, others who were missing the *skoupho*, others missing the schema, others missing the cassock, and some were in civilian clothes. Then I heard a voice next to me say: "This shows you what each one has taken away from the service."

He loved tradition, and abhorred worldly things and technological advancements. He was the representative of the monastery, and at the time the Athonite community was discussing building roads for cars on Athos. It was probably shortly before the millennial anniversary of the Holy Mountain. Father George was against it and did not sign, seeing far into the future and understanding quite correctly, as few did, that roads would destroy the Holy Mountain. Yet the roads came, and when he saw them opening a road to his monastery, Father George left and went to a place called Kerasia (Cherry-Tree) for a year and a half. A spiritual father counseled him there, saying: "You did well to leave, but I recommend you go back, because you may not have much time left, and I have seen many monks die miserable, far from their place of repentance."

He returned to his monastery and saw even more roads being built. He then said to himself, "I shall not leave the monastery, but while on Mount Athos I will never get into a car, as I am opposed to the roads that will destroy the Holy Mountain." And indeed, he put his words into action. When he was out in the world for the various affairs of the monastery, he would get into a car, but never on the Holy Mountain. He did not even get into a bus. When they had to go up the mountain for routine work, he would start off two hours earlier on a mule. And as representative he walked from Daphne to Karyes on foot. He had such exactness! And this exactness was taught to him by "*grigia*," which was a name by which he referred to the *Philokalia*, so that people would not know he read it.

Once, when he had a problem with a hernia, he visited a fellow Representative of his at Vatopedi and venerated the Holy Cincture of the Virgin Mary. He prayed, and the Panagia healed him. From then on, every year until he died, he went to the Feast of the Holy Cincture. At Vatopedi he did not want a cell or a bed. The fathers knew it and did everything in order to give him some rest, but he sat in a chair in the narthex for the whole vigil. He would begin the trip from his monastery the day before by boat, walk to Karyes with his carrier bag on his back, and walk from Karyes to Vatopedi on foot. After the vigil he would walk to Karyes, spend the night, and again walk down to Daphne to take the boat. He did this until 1997, when he was eighty-seven, as the next year he died.

When the monastery installed a kneading machine in the bakery, he never went into the bakery again, except for one time, when the baker pleaded with him to help because he was failing in baking the bread (as the elder had told him himself). He went in and with a single glance understood what the problem was. He counseled him and left.

In his cell he had only a clock, the tray on which he ate, and a cassock too dirty to be touched.

He did not allow them to put electricity or central heating in his cell. He kept his wood-burning stove, and the walls of his cell were completely black. He kept the door of the stove open, so that he could watch the fire, so it let out smoke and blackened the walls. He preferred to manually carry wood up the stairs rather than install central heating. He was against technological developments, the worldly spirit, and mindless comfort. He considered these things unsuitable and destructive for monks.

Although he was active and hardworking, he greatly loved silence. He would say, "The best companion for my soul is solitude." He was the representative, and so he often stayed in Karyes. Once, there was a twenty-seven-day period of constant fog, so thick that he could not even see the cherry-tree across the way from his window. The silence-loving Father George did not mind at all. He considered it a blessing, saying: "Those were the best days of my life. I just sat indoors and prayed on my prayer-rope."

A member of the Holy Community related that: "Of all the representatives, the one that made an impression on me was Father George from Saint Paul's. He was a very good monk and a man of prayer. When he was chairman, he would leave the office where everyone was sitting and go to the next office over to pray with the prayer-rope. When they called him to sign something, he would go, sign, and leave again to continue praying. He had discernment and nobility. When he did not agree with something for reasons of monastic conscience, he did not argue or become stubborn or try to impose his opinion."

Once, when he was serving as port master, four Germans came to receive hospitality. They had gotten lost coming from Dionysiou, and the monastery gates had closed. He received them, set out a table, and provided the best place for them to sleep. In the morning, they left full of joy. Even though he had suffered so much at the hands of the Germans, he forgot it all, since he was a genuine disciple of the Crucified one, who taught true, practical love, even towards one's enemies.

He made sure that every so often there would be a liturgy at the port. Sometimes he called the abbot (Father Andrew) or Father Gerasimus. As soon as the liturgy was over, he would make coffee for the others and with faith go up to to check the lines. He was certain, as he had prayed to Saint Demetrios (to whom the church at the porthouse was dedicated), and always anticipated a miracle. "Yesterday I made a prostration and asked Saint Demetrios for a small fish," he said, "and I caught a little grouper, just so big, so Saint Demetrios will host your meal today." The fathers were amazed at his faith, and he cooked it, as they gave glory to God and thanked the saint.

He was gracious and pleasant in his communication with others, telling his little jokes. He would tell a monk, "Could I please have two heads of garlic? I don't eat garlic, but I have high *piisi* ['poetry,' instead of *piesi*, 'blood pressure'], and they tell me that it helps with it." Another time he was not feeling well and said, "I hear that *iisi* ['arrogance,' instead of *iosi*, 'the flu'] is going around. Maybe I caught it also." Someone once scolded him saying, "Do you not know what you are saying?" To which he humbly answered, "Thank you very much father. I will not say it again."

He counseled someone who wanted to get thinner; "I will tell you what medication you need: motionlessness of the jaw. You will unquestionably lose weight."

He would also say from experience: "if you leave off going to the services, doing the prayer rule, and confessing, it is like putting grease on your shoes. The devil will slide you right out of the monastery."

He did not accept anything from anyone, whatever it may be, and when they asked him why, he would answer, "I found it in the Great Canon: 'He who receiveth gifts utterly destroyeth himself.'[3]" Once, while he was in town for some work, an elderly woman saw him with holes in his shoes and said to him, "Please, father, allow me to buy you a pair of shoes." He answered, "I am from a monastery that has shoes. There are other poor people; help them."

He lived completely detached with the entire meaning of the word. When he would go down to Athens for some affairs of the monastery,

3   Proverbs 15:27, in the reading of Wednesday before the Great Canon

he would not go by to see his mother who had been a widow from her youth. He would say, "I have renounced this world for Christ. If I go see my relatives, others must go as well." He did not go back on his monastic promises, nor did he become a reason for the others to transgress.

One time when he was accompanying a young monk to town to see a doctor, the young monk told him that he arranged with the abbot for his mother to come and see him. Father George answered: "Do as you have arranged with the elder, Father. Just beware. These things are ropes which hold the boat to shore. If we don't cut the ropes, the boat will be held here, and will not go forward."

Once, a lady from his village saw him in Athens and called for him:

"Father George!" He continued walking more quickly, but she ran, caught up with him, and asked: "Aren't you Father George?"

"Stop calling, blessed lady. Father George? Who is this Father George? You got confused."

"Ah, forgive me..." the lady said, shamefacedly walking away, and Father George continued on his way whispering to his companion, "Leave her be. We cannot get involved in conversation now; we have other work."

A pilgrim once asked him where he was from, and he answered wittily and simply, "I was born on a boat, I am not from anywhere." At the monastery, the pilgrim asked around and found out that this was Father George, who did not want anyone to know or engage him. Once, when Father George was serving as gardener, a certain pilgrim had become confused, lost the path and arrived at a dead end. He started calling for help, and Father George heard him and went to save him. Later, at Vespers, the man saw him and wanted to thank him, but Father George replied, "Me, sir? I do not know you. You've made a mistake," and disappeared.

When Father George passed his eightieth year, he would say, "I have passed over my strength; now what should I expect? From here on it is only toil and travail."[4]

<hr />

4   Psalm 89:10-11: "As for the days of our years, in their span they be threescore years and ten. And if we be in strength, mayhap fourscore years; and what is more

Only then did he stop working, and he would spend his days in the place where Maro heard the voice of the Panagia when she brought the Precious Gifts.[5] He would light the vigil-lamp and pray on his prayer-rope until Vespers. He put up a few corrugated tin sheets and some reeds for shelter, and he had a simple stool on which to sit. He wore a leather overcoat for the cold and sat there for hours on end saying the prayer, preparing for the great journey. He would say, "Father, what is Wednesday or Saturday to me? It will happen. I am not afraid at all."

He avoided speaking to passersby, sometimes acting foolishly to get them to leave him alone. A priest once asked him:

"Where are you from, Elder?"

"Eh, I am just passing by."

"Your name?"

"Squashseller."

Many times he stayed in the cemetery all night, praying, even in the coldest winter. One time the gatekeeper forgot to open the monastery's doors for the morning service, and Father George was knocking, waiting for him to open.

When the young monks would go to his cell and ask him if he wanted them to bring him anything, he asked only for them to leave him alone. "Why, Elder?" they would ask. "Because when you're alone, God sends three angels to be with you."

Until his old age he did not change cells, even though his was very high up and he had difficulty climbing the many stairs. In his last years he had nearly gone blind, and he went up by touch, leaning against the wall. He did not argue when they put a lamp in his cell so that he could see. He thanked them, saying, "At least now I can find my bed."

---

than these is toil and travail."

5   Maro, the mother of Sultan Mehmet the Conqueror, was bringing the Precious Gifts of the Magi to the Saint Paul's Monastery, which is at a short distance from the seashore. On the way, however, the Mother of God appeared to her and forbade her from advancing any further, since, as she said, "Here I am queen;" so Maro waited there until the fathers came and received the Gifts. Today at this spot there is a shrine.—ED.

In his final years he also suffered from his lower back, but he went down to the service every day. One day, during Orthros, the six Psalms had been read and Father George was still not there. The monk in charge of the elderly went up to check on him and found him sitting with a prayer-rope in his hand, deceased. It was the twenty-third of July 1998. They could not find any clothing of his own to dress him for burial, and so the fathers gave their own clothing and washed him for the first time since he became a monk.

Blessed is Father George, who with his unwashed body and humility preserved his spiritual wealth intact. He diligently managed to avoid the photographic lens, a difficult thing to accomplish living in a monastery for so many years, especially as representative and chairman in Karyes. On account of his humility, neither a photograph nor an identity card was found of him. Now let him rejoice and be glad there where he is, and may he forgive and pray for those who carelessly judged and underestimated him based on his external appearance.

May we have his blessing. Amen.

Ascetic Evthymius of Vigla and Lavra

Elder Evthymius was born in the year 1915 in the village of Gomati of Chalkidiki from Athanasius and Helen Papoutsi. In baptism
he was given the name Asterios. As a layman he worked and helped
his parents in their jobs, but he also liked music. He was gifted with
a good voice and he both played the viola and sang.

The grace of God enlightened him and he came to the Holy
Mountain to become a monk. In January of 1950 he began to live
communally in the monastery of Konstamonitou, where he became
a monk with the name Evthymius after the canonical novitiate. He
lived five to six years in the obedience of communal life and afterward
he desired the eremitic life. He told his thought to the elder and he
sent him into the forest to cut wood with an axe for one week without
food. The week passed and Elder Evthymius endured the trial. He
had a lot of strength and zeal, which lead him into the desert of Vigla
for greater struggles.

He became the disciple of a virtuous hieromonk and spiritual
father, the elder Barlaam, a former policeman, in the cell of Saints
Barlaam and Joasaph. Elder Evthymius would say about his elder that
he shone forth (with virtue) upon the whole Holy Mountain; "My
elder was holy," he would later explain and shed tears from emotion
and love.

There, Elder Evthymius gave himself over in obedience to Elder
Barlaam, to great ascetic feats. He fasted intensely, doing 'doubles';
that is, he would eat one plate of food without oil every two days. He
would go to the sea for his elder, fish and grant him repose as he was
old, but he himself savored the luxury of self-control, bread rusk and

legumes or cabbage boiled in water, without oil naturally. Together
with fasting he made countless prostrations and prayed ceaselessly.
He took care of the small area of their cell and did a little handiwork.
He learned to make spoons.

Struggling with such self-denial he did not delay to taste the fruits
of ascetic labor.

Through being occupied in prayer with insistence he had copious
tears when he was praying. One time he went to the Romanian Skete
for the liturgy and the monk in charge of the service went to tell him
to chant, but he saw the elder being choked by tears and out of piety
he did not speak to him.

For greater silence and unbroken progress in prayer he built a
small little cell right next to theirs with a built-in chair. There Elder
Evthymius would keep vigil saying the prayer. When he wanted to
rest, he would sleep sitting on his built-in chair, and again when he
awoke he continued his noetic work.

One Saturday, while he was praying with the prayer-rope to all
saints, he saw the archangel Michael, exactly as he is in a wall painting
in the Litya of the Catholikon of Lavra, with a sword and a woolen
cloak. "He was walking," he explained, "and the tail of his cloak was
opening and closing." He confessed this to his elder, who made the
sign of the cross and repeated, "Glory to Thee, O God."

Another time he was snatched up into theoria and saw the uncreated light. He revealed the secret to Elder Païsius who, in order
to benefit some young theologian and monk, mentioned the fact to
him. The young monk went to Elder Evthymius and was asking him
insistently with interest what happened, how he saw the uncreated
light, and if it is true that he was in theoria for one week. He tried to
avoid revealing his secret experience by saying to him, "Yes, my elder
gave me a penance of theoria for one week. We argued one time, I
thrashed him and he gave me this penance." The young monk naturally was astonished and did not manage to get to the bottom of the
matter with the ascetic of Vigla, Elder Evthymius.

Once he had buried his elder and taken his blessing, he continued
his ascetic struggles with greater intensity. Very few monks in our generation endure such great fasts. His life was dissimilar and inaccessible

Elder Evthymius of Vigla and Lavra

to the majority. His self-denial reached even to the point of willing martyrdom and death. One time he fasted eight days without food or water at all and became completely exhausted. He would say, "I should have died then; I had become like a raisin. I am still perplexed as to where water was found in my organism."

Together with his other labors he also played the fool quite wonderfully and effectively.

He would go to Philotheou back then when it was idiorhythmic, and when the monk in charge distributed the food supplies to the fathers, Elder Evthymius said to one monk, 'Now you'll see what I'll do to them.' He went and got in the front of the line before all the other fathers, and though he was not entitled to receive food, since he was not from the monastery, he said threateningly: "You will give me two cans of squid, a block of cheese, this and that", and when he had filled his sack with food, he went and distributed it to poor and helpless elders. He gave the impression of being strange, of being eccentric, of being crazy, of being greedy, yet he himself lived in extreme poverty and asceticism.

One time he had nailed a pulley to the wall of the Catholicon of Lavra. There he hung his three-hundred-knot prayer-rope, and while sitting in the church stall he would 'pull prayer-rope.' But the pulley would make noise while turning. One of the administrators of Lavra made a comment to him about it and Elder Evthymius gave him a slap.

He went to the feast of a certain cell and chanted. At the end he said commandingly to the elder of the brotherhood; "You will give me this and that and a mule to load it all and a monk to bring the mule back."

One time, when a boat with women came close to the shore, the elder drove them away by throwing rocks.

He gave money to a brotherhood to do forty-days liturgies for his parents who had fallen asleep, and afterward he went and asked for the money back, because, as he said, he saw them in hell.

He had a great voluntary poverty for Christ. His cassocks were patches on top of patches. No one would ever take them. They weren't even fit for scarecrows. His small little cell was old and simple but clean and tidy. Later on in life he left aside handiwork altogether and was occupied only with spiritual things. For money he had only two hundred drachmas and two or three liras in case some pauper passed by with 'absolutely nothing' so that he might give him alms.

When he went to Lavra to attend the liturgy and commune, he took back with him the food for the week. In order not to eat the bread of slothfulness, he served deftly in the dining hall.

He did not receive blessings at all. One pious lady from his village, who later became a nun, sent him a package with food, but the elder returned it to her. He had not gone to Karyes for perhaps more than half a century. When he was younger he went to the feasts and chanted sweetly and with emotion.

One time he went to a feast at Saint Paul's and saw a devil below the chandelier dancing.

Another time when he was younger, at a feast which he attended, he drank wine. Later a devil appeared, and from that time on he considered it good not to drink wine, a thing which he kept.

He was writing letters to his siblings and counseling them to repent and confess, but they were not giving any heed to his counsels. He invited them to come to the Holy Mountain so that he could speak to them about their salvation, but they were not interested. Then he wrote a false letter that he himself would die in a little and they must come quickly, to inherit his things, to take his liras, so that the Lavra would not get them. Then they immediately came to his cell and when they saw the situation and his poverty, they understood his ruse and departed in despair. "He didn't even have a bottle of wine, only dried bits of rusk", they said.

Many young monks sought to live with him, but no one was able to follow his ascetic program. Those that he wanted to kick out, because he saw they were not fit for this life, he made different trials of them and in this way they were forced to leave.

Saint Païsius said: "Elder Evthymius is similar to a doctor that gives very strong medicine to a patient. If he bears it, he is saved." That is to say, if someone goes near him and can follow him, he will be sanctified.

A hieromonk asked to live with him. He received him and told him to water the trees. Afterward, the hieromonk was waiting for him to set a table. Elder Evthymius said: "He thought that afterward I would wine and dine him. He said to me, 'I will leave,' 'You should leave now while there is light.' And so he left."

The elder himself was working in the summer without food and water, and moreover he was bare-chested in the sun, in order to place hardship upon himself.

Another hieromonk asked to live with him and Elder Evthymius wrote him the following letter:

> Elder Evthymius to Father ——: I greet you with a bow,
> You have bothered me many times to come to live in company. If, then, in truth you want us to live together for the rest of our lives, come, I receive you. And as I am now, as you know, I am not even able to discuss with men; you will have watch over the entire hermitage, and if you should find another person, you may have him as a helper for the liturgies and the rest of the needs; it will not be too bad. And if you ask me, with the help of God, I will not be wrong in whatever question you have. Should you give me a small piece of bread, I will be grateful. However I lived before I will live no longer. I have eaten my bread. Perhaps it may even be the will of God; I do not know, and for this reason I shall leave it to God and, whatever His will is, may it be done.
> Until now I have resisted and I did not keep anyone of those that passed through here. Now, I will leave it to God, and as He wishes let it be.
> Bowing, I greet you,
> Evthymius, Viglolavriotes

In the end, he did not go to live with him. And in this way, Elder Evthymius continued his struggle on his own. He was exact and not indulgent. He did not allow for any dispensation, neither for himself nor for him who would live with him. In 1985 he did the fast of the Apostles eating once every other day. He was seventy-two years old and the fast was a month long.

One time he provided hospitality for a young man who loved monasticism. He gave him the room of his elder to sleep in. The covers were clean but torn to shreds. In between he placed nylon to keep them from dissolving.

The speed, the zeal, the forcefulness, and the flexibility of the elder when he did prostrations in the Church made an impression on the youth. He seemed like a trained athlete; despite his seventy years Elder Evthymius was an athlete for Christ. It was Great Lent. He read a part of the service with a magnifying glass in his hand, since his sight had already weakened. His cassocks were patched and fraying but clean. He wore a hood and monastic hat of his own creation while in church. Even his appearance, his schema, and his way of life were unusual, just as he himself came across as unusual to others. But his eccentricities hid a spiritual understanding.

After Vespers he set table. He offered the best he had so as to grant comfort to his guest: boiled chickpeas without oil, wetted bread rusk, and two types of olives. "These olives are better", he said. But both of them were extremely bitter. The plates were earthenware, the table old, the kitchen half dark, with a dirt floor, but everything went well together; they had an ascetic grace.

Afterward in discussion the elder was fatherly and affectionate; he counseled the visitor very nicely and practically. He was speaking with a certain freedom, with dispassion, with bright eyes, similar to the brightness of heaven; he showed the innocence of a child.

In his hut, everything was simple; you would not find anything new. They transported you to a bygone era, even his few books. He had the Philokalia in a single volume from the first publication. But even he himself felt that he lived in a different era. Or rather, from a different era he came into our generation. After leaving, his visitor wrote him a letter, thanking him for his hospitality equal to Abraham, and sent him a few envelopes and sheets of paper. The returned them. Even on this point he kept exactness.

With the passing of time his strength failed. He felt weak and had difficulty going to the Liturgies, not only to Lavra but also to the Romanian skete. But he did not change his asceticism and his rule. He would say, "Now I am eating once a day, and twice in Bright week." He said one time, "Would that I could make a little cell at Kyr-Isaiah and take on a way of life," that is, to begin with ascetic struggles.

And so, he was forced on account of old age and weakness to live in the coenobium of Lavra. He had already lost his hearing and sometimes he would sign 'Evthymius the deaf'. Later on he also became blind because he did not want to go out into the world for a surgery. He broke his leg and did not want to go out for any reason.

At the Lavra, he followed the typicon and was careful not to eat anything outside of the refectory.

In the year 2001, at the age of eighty-six, he did a three day fast but secretly, because the nurse monk would not allow him. He said affectedly, "Now I am going, I am no longer able. At one point I did such things." But he managed, despite his age, to do a three-day fast.

One Clean Monday, while he was in the chapel of the Holy Trinity, he heard a demon yelling to the others, "Gather together, we have a war".

Many people visited him in the hospital, in order to hear his counsels. He would say: "The whole foundation is fasting. From here all the other things are brought forth: prayer, obedience, vigils. When a man fasts, the intellect acquires strength and conquers the evil thoughts. He hears the prayer, 'Lord Jesus Christ, have mercy on me' inside of him. The body of the old man does not fear eating once a day. Eating once a day (that is for someone to eat once a day after Vespers) is not effective when one sits around all day; it needs work, it also requires work. When a man fasts for two days and beyond, then he can set aside work."

"A monk should not open up too many cares. He should secure those basic needs and should remain undisturbed; he should not have passionate attachments. Then, whatever he does, the fruit remains. With distraction, forgetfulness and ignorance come like a sponge and soak up from the mind whatever one reads or whatever spiritual thing one hears. Many are leaving from the coenobium in order to do their will. There are six responsibilities of a disciple to an elder. They are written in the Athonite booklet" (the service of the Athonite Fathers).

Elder Evthymius wanted for a monk, especially an anchorite, to be an ascetic, a faster. He believed that "the beasts of the passions are slain by fasting". He wrote to a young man who loved monasticism and was serving in the army: "Although thoughts are imposing upon you to make a three-day fast, you should not listen to them. Fast until the ninth hour every day and until Vespers you should not take anything, not even antidoron". As he was living and struggling, in this way he counseled, and he imagined that others could do nearly the same asceticism. He was even brought to being undiscerning by his extreme zeal and fighting spirit.

Elder Evthymius, while giving all his being to his ascetic struggle and using 'severity' for the cleansing of the passions, lived decades on his own, wherefore he would sometimes sign, 'the desert dweller'. He not only went without material comforts but even avoided contact with men. He lived extremely isolated, without friends, acquaintances, fellow initiates. This perhaps did not benefit him, because he acquired a certain suspicion, on account of which he quarreled with some and was argumentative, if, of course, this was not related to his affected foolishness. But we pray that the good God in the face of his great sacrifice for the love of Christ not penalize this small human weakness.

His life is a silent witness and a censure for the indolent majority of the monks of our generation but also an example for imitation. In his last years, Elder Evthymius, while sitting in the hospital of the Lavra, deaf and blind, kept his fasting despite being over ninety years old and was asking, when they offered him food, if it was from the dining hall. Whatever was not from the dining hall he did not eat. He fasted until the ninth hour every day and only on Tuesday and weekends did he make a dispensation for oil. He did not leave off the prayer at any time. Although he was in bed he was holding his prayer-rope that he had hung from a pulley nailed to the wall.

To whomever asked him he gave practical and beneficial counsels, while he himself was preparing for the great journey. He was praying constantly for himself and the world. He would often say,

"What should I do? I do not have enough tears to weep for the world."

Someone made mention to him of a bishop that had done away with the impediments to the priesthood. Elder Evthymius answered, "He needs to be tied to the jetty and executed by a firing squad." He made mention of a certain district and the other one was amazed, because he understood that the elder perceived which bishop it was.

To another monk that visited him, he described in detail the other's cell without having been there.

In the infirmary of the monastery he remembered some people that had caused him much troubled and he began to criticize and condemn them, with the result that the grace of God abandoned him. His prayer was cut off and he sank down into a state of despair. For six months he endured, living in hell. The fathers that served him understood the cause of the temptation and summoned the fathers with whom Elder Evthymius had difficulties. They forgave each other and gradually he was completely restored and once again found both peace and the prayer.

Sensing his departure beforehand, he forgave all the fathers and fell asleep peacefully on the ninth of July in the year 2004.

May we have his blessing. Amen.

UNCUT MOUNTAIN PRESS TITLES

Books by Archpriest Peter Heers

Fr. Peter Heers, *The Ecclesiological Renovation of Vatican II: An Orthodox Examination of Rome's Ecumenical Theology Regarding Baptism and the Church*, 2015

Fr. Peter Heers, *The Missionary Origins of Modern Ecumenism: Milestones Leading up to 1920*, 2007

The Works of our Father Among the Saints, Nikodemos the Hagiorite

Vol. 1: *Exomologetarion: A Manual of Confession*

Vol. 2: *Concerning Frequent Communion of the Immaculate Mysteries of Christ*

Vol. 3: *Confession of Faith*

Other Available Titles

Elder Cleopa of Romania, *The Truth of our Faith, Vol. I: Discourses from Holy Scripture on the Tenants of Christian Orthodoxy*

Elder Cleopa of Romania, *The Truth of our Faith, Vol. II: Discourses from Holy Scripture on the Holy Mysteries*

Fr. John Romanides, *Patristic Theology: The University Lectures of Fr. John Romanides*

Demetrios Aslanidis and Monk Damascene Grigoriatis, *Apostle to Zaire: The Life and Legacy of Blessed Father Cosmas of Grigoriou*

Protopresbyter Anastasios Gotsopoulos, *On Common Prayer with the Heterodox According to the Canons of the Church*

Robert Spencer, *The Church and the Pope*

G. M. Davis, *Antichrist: The Fulfillment of Globalization*

St. Gregory Palamas, *Apodictic Treatises on the Procession of the Holy Spirit*

St. Hilarion Troitsky, *On the Dogma of the Church: An Historical Overview of the Sources of Ecclesiology*

Fr. Alexander Webster and Fr. Peter Heers, Editors, *Let No One Fear Death*

Subdeacon Nektarios Harrison, *Metropolitan Philaret of New York: Zealous Confessor for the Faith*

Elder George of Grigoriou, *Catholicism in the Light of Orthodoxy*

Archimandrite Ephraim Triandaphillopoulos, *Noetic Prayer as the Basis of Mission and the Struggle Against Heresy*

Select Forthcoming Titles

Nicholas Baldimtsis, *Life and Witness of St. Iakovos of Evia*

Georgio, *Errors of the Latins*

Fr. Peter Heers, *Going Deeper in the Spiritual Life*

Abbe Guette, *The Papacy*

Athonite Fathers of the 20th Century, Vol. II

This 1ˢᵗ Edition of

ATHONITE FATHERS OF THE 20ᵀᴴ CENTURY

written by the Cell of the Resurrection on the Holy Mountain, with a cover design by George Weis, typeset in Baskerville, and printed in this two thousand and twenty second year of our Lord's Holy Incarnation, is one of the many fine titles available from Uncut Mountain Press, translators and publishers of Orthodox Christian theological and spiritual literature. Find the book you are looking for at

u n c u t m o u n t a i n p r e s s . c o m

GLORY BE TO GOD
FOR ALL THINGS

AMEN.

Made in United States
Troutdale, OR
12/21/2023

16252131R00136